ABOUT THE AUTHOR

— my best friend, wife, and business partner, Melissa —

Melissa is too humble to introduce herself, so I volunteered to do that for her. Most people who start a company at age 23 with their 25 year old boyfriend and turn that into an enterprise the TODAY Show called *"the Gold Standard for early childhood play"* would feel content they've made their contribution to society. But that isn't the case with Melissa. Although our toy company Melissa & Doug has touched millions of children, Melissa longs to connect with people in a more direct and personal way. By sharing her story of salvation, Melissa welcomes us deep inside her soul and takes us on her journey, revealing how her *Life*Lines transformed despair into a beacon of hope. Who would ever guess Melissa, who seemingly lives a charmed and carefree life, begins many days the same way far too many others do, wondering if she'll make it to tomorrow? Melissa shows us that when darkness descends, and it seems there's no escape, there actually *is* a way out, there actually *is* hope, and there actually *is* a path that can lead to meaning and purpose. For 30+ years, Melissa's toys have brought smiles and joy to families everywhere, yet this book — authentic, unedited, and in her own words — is her greatest gift yet. I can't wait for the rest of the world to be inspired by Melissa the same way I have been since our very first date in the summer of 1986.

—

Doug

*Life*Lines

*Life*Lines

*An inspirational journey from
profound darkness to radiant light*

Melissa Bernstein

*Life*Lines

We welcome all seekers to join our community at
www.*Life*Lines.com

To personally connect with Melissa, please email her at
MelissaBernstein@*Life*Lines.com

Graphic Design by *Erica Jago*

LIBRARY OF CONGRESS

Name: Bernstein, Melissa B., author.

*Title: Life*Lines : *an inspirational journey from profound darkness to radiant light*
Melissa Bernstein.

Description: Westport, CT: *Life*Lines, LLC, 2021.

Identifiers: LCCN: 2020918834 | ISBN: 978-1-7354397-0-9 (Hardcover)

Subjects: LCSH Bernstein, Melissa B. | Bernstein, Melissa B.--Mental health. |
Mental health--Anecdotes. | Business women--United States--Biography. |
Anxiety--Alternative treatment. | Poetry, American. | Happiness. | Conduct of life. |
Self-acceptance. | Mental healing. | BISAC BIOGRAPHY & AUTOBIOGRAPHY / Personal
Memoirs | SELF-HELP / Motivational & Inspirational | SELF-HELP / Personal Growth /
Happiness | POETRY / Subjects & Themes / General

Classification: LCC BF575.S37 B48 2021
DDC 646.7/092--dc23

Printed in Canada

FIRST EDITION

@seek*Life*Lines

To those souls who took their lives
Convinced the world would never care
And the ones who keep on fighting
For a pathway through despair

Doug—for 35 years you have been the lemonade to my lemons, the silver lining in my dark clouds, and the lighthouse in my stormy seas. Thank you for being an unwavering source of strength, optimism, and hope.

All these decades orchestrating
This impassioned symphony
Weaving overwhelming joy
With waves of abject misery
Forge the tale of my existence
Ringing powerful and true
And beseeching liberation
So the world can hear it too

*Life*Lines

CONTENTS

Why now?

Here I was, in my fifth decade of life yet still believing I was a visitor from another planet who would never be understood or embraced here on Earth. From early on I knew something was awry within my being, wallowing in a continual sense of unease and profound unsettledness in my soul. This induced scathing criticism from others for being so odd and ultimate rejection by those I desperately sought to befriend. Yet despite these judgments I still invariably fought to disguise my eccentricities and fit in, never finding mass acceptance and becoming deeply isolated and bitterly resentful. And then, seemingly out of the blue through a handful of random dots connecting by sheer coincidence, I woke up out of the lifelong stupor to see I wasn't alone at all. After an eternity of asking the question *"why"* and drowning in a sea of despair, I witnessed a lifeline descending through the murky water beckoning me to grab hold, rise up, and witness my very first glimpse of light. For I had finally been handed the key to unlock my essence, with every answer sought now bountifully displayed before me.

The first *"dot"* came in reading the book *"Man's Search for Meaning"* by Victor Frankl. At its conclusion Frankl mentioned research he initiated post-ordeal in logotherapy, a form of *"existential analysis."* Although priding myself on possessing a wide vocabulary, I had never before heard the word *"existential"* and was curious to its meaning. And when its definition, *"...a philosophy according to which the world has no meaning and each person is alone and completely responsible for his or her own actions"* (Cambridge Dictionary) permeated my brain, a lightning bolt penetrated my heart, as I was literally reading an explanation of my innermost ruminations.

In fact, I almost believed someone was playing a cruel joke on me as the concepts of existentialism were so akin to my perceptions that I could hardly digest the enormity of this revelation. It was unfathomable to learn *"existential depression"* could precisely detail behavior which for decades seemed so unusual and stigmatizing. Because this potentially meant I wasn't alone in my anguish, and there were others like me in the world!

As I researched further and learned about those suffering existential depression, I saw a very high percentage of them were exceedingly creative. In fact, reading the following sentence made the entire universe grind to a halt: *"It is probable that people who are the most thoughtful, curious, and creative are primarily the ones who experience existential depression"* (JAMES THURMAN WEBB, psychologist and author). This insight brought me to my knees, for just a handful of creators thought to have experienced existential depression included: Wolfgang Mozart, Vincent Van Gogh, Ludwig Van Beethoven, Emily Dickinson, Michelangelo, Sir Isaac Newton, T.S. Eliot, William Faulkner, Fyodor Dostoyevsky, Leo Tolstoy, Charles Dickens, Edgar Allen Poe, Ernest Hemingway, Winston Churchill, Hans Christian Anderson, Sylvia Plath and Virginia Woolf. And while by no means was I comparing or elevating myself to these individuals' prolific levels of creativity, I felt heartfelt communion in sharing the same source of misery birthing art. Perhaps the most sobering realization, however, was that several of these individuals couldn't handle the mania's toll and tragically took their lives, signifying the unrelenting nature

"It is probable that people who are the most thoughtful, curious, and creative are primarily the ones who experience existential depression."

JAMES THURMAN WEBB,
PSYCHOLOGIST AND AUTHOR

of this affliction. Yet despite its magnitude, this epiphany
gave me the validation needed in perceiving I was not alone.
For until now, no one had known the depths of my despair
or understood that what I experienced didn't just end or get
better, which made this newfound awareness enlightening
yet terrifying. There was a very fine line between bearing its
burden or perishing beneath its weight.

With the recognition that I might not be entirely alone in the
world dawned a profound awakening. It was unfortunately
occurring at age fifty, but was a rebirth nonetheless in
allowing me to see myself clearly for the first time. I
now saw existential depression as the heavy cloud I lived
under, shaping my world view and making me feel so desolate
and distinct from others. With this realization also came
the knowledge I had a particular personality type fostering
this type of depression. Comprehending a causal reason
for my relentless malaise filled me with the awe of a
child finally discovering where she fit in the world. For it
was clear that every day I survived was a victory, because I
was fighting a demon trying to strangle me. And my fervent
need to create was necessary to wrest meaning from the
meaninglessness of existence and channel pain into tangible
form or I would be extinguished by despair.

Learning I suffered from existential depression was only the
beginning of this journey to self-discovery. For although
providing an initial glimpse into the derivation of anguish,
it still didn't explain the very nature of my personality in

also possessing innumerable quirks kept repressed from the world. But in researching existential depression the next "*dot*" emerged, and I was finally able to unlock reasons behind these unusual characteristics. For it appeared most who experienced existential depression were also highly sensitive individuals exhibiting strong personality traits. Kazimierz Dabrowski (1902-1980) spent his lifetime studying the mental health of intellectually and artistically inclined children and adults, recognizing that extreme intensity of their emotions and sensitivities was actually part of their psycho-physical makeup.

Dabrowski's research disclosed that individuals who both suffered from existential depression and were highly creative often had excessive levels of reactivity in their central nervous systems called over-excitabilities (referred to as OEs). This alertness stimulated their nervous systems to a much higher degree than others', with the tendency to remain in those heightened states for extensive periods of time. And not surprisingly, these qualities were generally viewed as over-reactive and attention-seeking to those without acute sensitivities. In fact Dabrowski, in his clinical practice, saw many creative artists and writers undergoing profound spiritual crises. This forged his primary mission to "*save and protect those who were tuned to the pain of the world and its dangerous trends, but whose voice was not heeded*" (MICHAEL M. PIECHOWSKI, *Experiencing in a Higher Key. Gifted Education Communicator, Spring* 2002). "*He saw those who were open to higher realities were often poorly adapted to this world and thus at risk for not succeeding or even surviving*" (MICHAEL M. PIECHOWSKI, *Mellow Out, They Say. If Only I Could, page* 18).

Dabrowski's OEs produced extreme sensitivity, awareness and intensity to life and life experiences so distinct they fell into five categories: imaginational, emotional, intellectual, sensual and psycho-motor. This newfound opportunity to explore my innate being left me awestruck, with the answers I had been seeking now plainly manifested to behold. For these traits were indeed a dictionary definition of my personality with every peculiarity accurately delineated. Could it actually be true? After 50 years of believing I was an utter misfit, were there truly others experiencing similar sensitivities? Was I not in fact the only one who ever sobbed "*I feel too much*" and then suffered the criticism, "*you're too overly reactive and emotional—can't you just calm down and act normal?*" I then proceeded to purchase the only few books available on the subject, discovering individuals may experience OEs in just one or more of these five categories to be classified "*highly sensitive.*" But here was the kicker: my personality mirrored the exact descriptions of all five OEs, at long last substantiating the extent of my agitation. It was almost inconceivable that an immense picture window had finally opened into my soul.

Seeing myself in this new light of having a combination of both existential depression and hypersensitivities/OEs was truly revelatory. Suddenly every single emotion and fear I had experienced throughout the decades made complete sense. There was no more mystery of who I was and why I acted in certain ways, for it was apparent I had been born with a particular personality type and thus exhibited certain reflective attributes. And although terrifying in its enormity, it was an incredible relief to have an explanation for what seemed such a lifelong mystery. I now understood why I always struggled in vain to fit in, never finding true acceptance. Perhaps my people existed somewhere—but certainly not where I had been looking throughout life. And if at age 50 I was just starting to understand myself in connecting dots independently, then there must be other Melissas out there drowning in despair and needing a lifeline. For my people were surely not basking in the light, but either quietly creating in the shadows, locked in anguish unable to leave home, or masking their differences from the world without daring to expose their honest selves. I now looked forward, though with a fair measure of trepidation, to examining each OE and discovering what made me tick. For if I could solve the puzzle of my own life then perhaps I could help others do the same.

But that said, why would I ever risk exposure at this late stage by transcribing my deepest, darkest fears and struggles on paper for all to see? For despite a lifetime of internal angst I had reached the epitome of *"success"* by conventional standards: co-founding a $450 million toy company, forging a wonderful marriage to my best friend and business partner Doug, raising six wonderful children and living a charmed life with greater material rewards than ever imagined. Yet despite my shiny exterior, I still desperately yearned to be accepted for who I truly was. For no matter how intently I tried to suppress that wanting through the bustling, activity-filled days of my life, the inner cry of my soul *"to be seen"* was becoming deafening. And I was no longer willing to lurk in the shadows living a lie. Every molecule of my being now demanded freedom to disclose that despite living with

darkness, despair and the relentless drumbeat of mortality
pounding in my head, I had still miraculously discovered a way
to channel pain into positivity and live meaningfully. And
having found salvation, I now hoped to encourage others
to do the same through embracing their essence without
'fixing' or 'changing' themselves. Because with fifty years spent
assimilating, denying, repressing and living the life of an
imposter, I knew wholly accepting ourselves was the only path
to finding fulfillment.

If I was just now exposing and embracing my truth after decades
of despising myself and nearly taking my life, then there must
be others locked in the throes of despair unable to break
free. Because it was simply a fluke to learn that what I had
tried to mask, morph and destroy my entire life were actually
the very qualities giving me the ability to create. So perhaps
hearing my message might forge a sense of kinship and
connection with similar souls, allowing them to move forward
with newfound purpose. For I knew my mission was to now
help others unearth what gave their lives meaning and find the
outlet to express it to the world, making light from dark and
connection from isolation.

This is what brings me to today and this discourse you are
about to read. Throughout my life I documented the beauty,
darkness and incongruity of life through words, yet kept
them shrouded certain they were much too simple, despairing
and personal to touch others. Despite that fact, I quenched
my fervent need to create through other channels—
conceiving nearly 10,000 children's products over thirty

years along with innumerable crafts, photos, jewelry and
parenting/entrepreneurship blogs and articles. Yet although
I was still creating, there remained a gaping hole in my soul
as I was desperate to be seen in darkness as well as light.
And that lifelong collection of words, more than any other
medium, honestly represented my duality and authentic self.
I would never find solace until these *Life*Lines and guiding
beacons emerged from the shadows to bask in the glow of
acceptance and touch others.

I therefore embarked on the most terrifying journey of my
life—turning five decades of verses and journal writings into the
volumes before you. For although I had finally accepted living
with despair and would no longer feel shame or wallow in pity,
I would remain incomplete until the reflections keeping me
alive all these years were liberated to connect with others. My
profound hope is reading these raw disclosures held captive for
ages will give you strength to escape your prison and find solace
as well. For then neither of us shall remain alone, linked to
a much larger, enduring force beyond ourselves. I am humbled
and thankful to share my most vulnerable confessions with
you now.

CREATIVITY—*All forms*

*From my earliest
memories I felt different
than everyone else and
not in a special way—
different in a weird,
eccentric way confirming
I would never
find acceptance.*

I entered this world an agitated, churning, distressed being. In fact, although my mother lamented I had terrible colic as a baby and was unable to be soothed, I was clearly just lashing out at my inability to feel a sense of belonging in the world I had been thrust. From my earliest memories I felt different than everyone else and not in a special way—different in a weird, eccentric way confirming I would never find acceptance. And this sense of abnormality wasn't alleviated by the fact I asked a lot of "why" questions, but not the why questions of a content, curious soul eager to explore the world in all its wonder. These were the why questions of an already desperate toddler hearing an incessant drumbeat that the hands of time were ticking away with her powerless to stop their march. That cloud of impending doom made me insistent on knowing the purpose of life if we were ultimately bound to die and turn to dust, and specifically why I had been put on this earth and what I was meant to do while here. And given I never received adequate answers, was left helpless to under-stand or control terrors unable to be seen or expressed.

My paramount goal each day became resolving existential questions and deriving meaning amidst the bleakness so my brain could find solace. Long before it could be comprehended or articulated, expressing inexplicable feelings through organic conception became my innate method of deciphering life's incongruities and quelling suffocating agony.

This manifested itself in a steady stream of words,
notes and later ideas (which eventually became
products) perpetually running through my head—a
ticker tape flowing between my eyebrows and the top
of my skull. The words in particular were frustratingly
headstrong—frenzied, raucous and beseeching me
to reach up, grab hold, and pull them down to be
transcribed, or threatening to disappear into oblivion.
I tried heeding their plea by scrawling them onto
whatever was at my disposal—notebooks, toilet paper,
napkins, my skin, walls and scraps of paper I later found
shoved in pockets or socks, between my mattress and
box spring or strewn beneath my bed. But although
I wished to suppress these words since their ferocity
and darkness were terrifying, they were relentless in
demanding freedom and unwilling to surrender. The
analogy I envisioned in restraining them was sitting
on an overly filled suitcase (my brain) and attempting
to zip it shut as its contents (the words) were fleeing
from every egress. For I was instinctively impelled
to submerge the incessant chatter, as the burden of
recording its perpetual flow was overwhelming and
destroyed my efforts to lead a normal life and fit in.

In truth, I hoped if I denied the existence of these words
they would eventually vanish and allow my head to clear.
But unfortunately such rejection brought no relief as I
ended up feeling perpetual guilt in denying them "life."
I did, unequivocally, believe all conceptualizations to be
living, breathing beings if I chose to birth them through

transference onto paper or into form. Their fate was
entirely in my hands since I was master and could set
them free, or act as prison guard holding them captive
in the dungeon of my mind to perish. This *"power"* could
have made me feel omnipotent, but as neither ignoring
nor transcribing concepts brought perceptible relief I
remained in constant turmoil. For in truth I felt a tragic
sense of loss when a melody, verse or idea ran through
my head, was neglected, and then quickly evaporated
into the depths of obscurity to never rise again, or when
a rhyme or song emerged from my imagination and was
swiftly captured, but then immediately squirreled away
to remain in eternal darkness. Neither brought any
measure of comfort or closure.

It so happened my conceptions were quite basic in
nature and arose in entirely finished forms. The words
appeared in complete verse and always rhymed, the
melodies surfaced wholly composed, and the products
emerged fully conceived as well. I merely rendered
them precisely as envisioned and they just "*made sense.*"
And although my everyday thoughts and questions
were incredibly deep, dark, despairing and truly too
weighty to be plainly discussed or answered, the verses
and tunes I wrote (and products I ultimately created)
came out simple and innocent as those of a child.
I found that naiveté frustrating and never understood
why I couldn't express myself more intellectually or
profoundly, yet never received that answer since my
content remained unexposed. Truly no one in my first

three decades knew I saw these conceptions in my head and detailed them on countless bits of paper, mainly because virtually everything emanating was too horribly bleak and depressing to be shared. It was nothing I could proudly display and boast, *"Look what I made,"* for I already felt a complete misfit and didn't want that magnified through revealing these somber creations. So although I penned many hundreds of verses and songs over the years, they stayed locked away in a desk drawer unseen and unheard. I therefore never experienced joy in the kinship of creation, petrified others would catch a glimpse of the omnipresent darkness and further ostracize me. Moreover, the moment one verse or song exited my brain another swiftly filled its place, making it impossible to rest easy.

For years I simply forged more darkness from darkness. And although the innate angst was continually channeled into creative outlets and tangible form, it never brought solace since it didn't answer the questions: *"Why am I here, and what is the absolute meaning of life?"* Furthermore, the shame over revealing such malaise rendered me unable to forge connection and purpose. My creative output was entirely veiled in secrecy, having penned ruminations without a soul knowing and then burying them in a hole where they'd never be seen again. Emptying my head was just a chore necessary to ensure it wouldn't overflow—similar to dumping the trash. And I slogged

I had evolved from hearing the drumbeat of mortality pounding in my head to now hearing the laughter of children ringing in my heart.

through knowing it was my duty, but without joy or intention in doing so.

However, the day I brainstormed an innovative line of children's puzzles from that very same despair was when my life began to change. For the first time ever I felt something entirely different—having spent a lifetime suffocating with a tube suddenly jammed into my trachea and experiencing what it meant to breathe fresh air. I was no longer creating anguished verses or songs too humiliating to share, but uplifting, joyous, tangible toys able to touch real people and impact lives through inspiring play. I had evolved from hearing the drumbeat of mortality pounding in my head to now hearing the laughter of children ringing in my heart.

Channeling pain into more pain cloaked in darkness had effectively disabled me from finding communion or meaning in creation. But with power to now funnel desolation into engaging playthings for children, I was resuscitated from my lifelong coma. Suddenly every excruciating emotion made sense and a lifetime of sorrow swelled with purpose. And I knew it was imperative to morph pain into positivity and derive meaning through creation the rest of my days for it to perpetually make sense. I would transform every ounce of misery into tangible products able to stir hearts and foster genuine connections.

Until now I had no empowering means of expression, with countless feelings imprisoned and no idea
what they meant or how to set them free. Hence my
heart became so rife with sadness I was certain it would
explode through my chest. This led to profound
depression. And ultimately, this tangled mass
of emotion had nowhere to go but into more
darkness, pushing me even further within myself.
When the burden of those feelings grew too great my
hands would shake, my head pound, my heart race and
I'd become weak with exhaustion—paralyzed by
the futility of life. But now, finally, I had my
creative pathway leading out of obscurity into the
blazing sunshine.

Once I had my lifeline it was as if a massive faucet had
opened leading from my brain through my heart and
then directly out my hands. I just kept channeling that
force into new toys—hundreds of them per year for the
next three decades, and so many on the back list my
biggest fear became there were not enough years left
to see them to fruition. I had proven darkness could
transform into light and there was no greater freedom.
And most importantly, I realized I actually controlled the
creation process as well, which was revelatory. I could
choose to create darkness out of darkness, or light
out of darkness. Likewise, that meant I could decide
whether to remain miserable from churning out dark,
despairing content, or live in peace by funneling anguish

into positivity and vibrant designs. It was entirely my
choice. And how appropriate to have selected toys
as my conduit, which held more promise than any
medium I could have possibly envisioned.

Almost overnight I felt utter liberation in my creative
pursuits with no anxiety, since my two most externally
criticized oddities—a very naïve and simplistic view
of the world, plus an incessant need to question
and rabidly search for answers—catalyzed to forge
our initial playthings. I determined to thoroughly
assess our early categories of wooden puzzles and
manipulatives by researching them from the beginning
of time, spending months in museums and libraries
documenting their history and devouring every
morsel with insatiable curiosity. I believed knowledge
was power, and the better I understood a segment
the more opportunities would naturally present
themselves in seeing untapped niches, improvements
on existing products, executional flaws in packaging
and merchandising, pricing disparities and potential
to reinvent lackluster play patterns. These "*solutions*"
wouldn't necessarily present themselves immediately,
but often take weeks or perhaps even months of
data amalgamating within to emerge. But for some
reason as insecure as I was in navigating life, I had
tremendous faith in the creative process—certain if
I wholly internalized observations and let those
revelations distill throughout my being, then the

creative path would become clear. And if that
path didn't become imminently evident there was likely
no pathway to be found. I never once second-guessed
that intuition, because I somehow just instinctively
knew it was correct.

The metaphor I envisioned in the journey of product
creation was standing at the edge of a deep, dark forest
holding a simple concept or *"spark"* in my hands—but
the forest was so dense I couldn't find the pathway
to the other side and was terrified of entering. Yet
I knew on the other side of that barricade were
millions and millions of consumers waiting for me
with outstretched arms—eager to embrace my product
as long as I could find the pathway through and
present it to them. My objective, therefore, was to
somehow access that clear path—which represented the
odyssey of turning an *"idea"* into a completely finished
product consumers were clamoring to purchase. That
process involved determining how to make a product
more enticing and a better solution than anything on
the market, becoming the juice that got me up in the
morning and intoxicating me like nothing else.

One might presume ideating and developing entirely
new toy categories would induce tremendous
pressure—especially when that meant the growth of our
company was resting on my shoulders. But thankfully
toy concepts seemed to flow out of me as naturally as
breathing, and for the first time ever I had something

*Creating products
and the creative
process were sheer
bliss—no longer
constrained in a
limited body but
soaring miles
above with the
boundless potential
of invention.*

special to offer the world. I guess this was the definition of finding one's sweet spot and feeling pure, unadulterated liberation with the ability to morph anguish to luminous form. Creating products (in whatever fashion they emerged) and the creative process, it turned out, were sheer bliss—no longer constrained in a limited body but soaring miles above with the boundless potential of invention. With such newfound freedom it was exhilarating arriving at work each morning, tingling with the promise of where the infinite realm of imagination might take me. And the more I was actively involved in starting from a blank canvas and finishing with a vibrant plaything touching multitudes of children, the greater my joy and sense of contentment.

In the light of this newfound knowledge that creating was actually my unique path to finding meaning and purpose, I understood my separation from the rest of the world was actually not a flaw to be despised, but a special quality making me unique. Perhaps my difference was what allowed me to create—which I now understood was the greatest joy possible. Could it actually be true? For decades I had never seen it as such, but maybe the dots were finally connecting and creation was actually my lifeline *out* of despair! Yet throughout my life I had *never* felt special in any way, with my sole mission to singularly emulate those around me. And I had failed miserably in doing so—incapable of mirroring the popular people I most admired and left without anything to hold dear or embrace as my own.

I struggled desperately to fit in and never succeeded—
an isolated misfit destined to never find her way out
of misery. Under this dense fog the words, songs and
products flowing out of me were nothing more than
nuisances needing ridding since they clogged my head,
clamored to be released, and required expulsion to
maintain sanity. But I clearly wasn't proud of them
or thinking I was doing anything worthy in setting
them free. However this spark of insight was like
the nascent bud of a flower, opening to reveal other
incredible insights about who I was and the derivation
of my anguish. And thankfully so, since before this
revelation I had tremendous difficulty maintaining
hope in a world seeming utterly hopeless and
rejecting me at every turn.

Creating had become my pathway out of despair in
connecting to the freedom of my imagination, no
longer struggling to conform to what society defined
as success and deemed acceptable. I was free as a bird
when inventing in the magnitude of possibility, in my
ultimate flow and complete state of euphoria. White
space held the power of potential and promise—only
constrained by what our imaginations could conceive
and a launch pad to innovation furthering humanity.
Pyramids could be built, symphonies composed
and space travel made reality from the blank canvas
of imagination. I found that power absolutely
intoxicating, for I was so restricted in my own body
and imprisoned by the austere walls of my head fearing

what it couldn't control. But white space lifted me
beyond the cage into expansiveness flush with purpose.
I felt invincible in the ability of my mind to design
whatever it envisioned, knowing there was nothing
more vital to achieving fulfillment.

I truly reveled in experiencing no disappointment
or disillusionment in creation, since the process was
entirely mine to govern. Being master of these sparks'
fate and my decision whether they were kindled or not
was empowering when juxtaposed against my inability
to affect the ephemerality of existence. And once I
stopped fighting to repress darkness there was a never-
ending torrent of expression waiting to be freed and
transform into palpable content. I now felt tremendous
urgency to expel these notions as rapidly as possible,
petrified they would either evaporate or I would expire
before forging them into worthy offerings.

My final sobering realization was the price I paid for
creativity was living with depression. The reason I was
able to create was because of exactly who I was—with
my hyper-sensitivities and over-excitabilities catalyzing
to forge content. So if the cost of innovation was the
despair that birthed it, I either needed to be grateful and
accepting of that burden or choose to end it all, since it
was simply too exhausting to keep resisting. Honestly,
I had never seen it that way before—but understanding
it in this manner was truly liberating. I had always
despised myself for being so intense, sensitive, deep and

Channel darkness into light and forge meaning through connecting with others.

morose, wanting nothing more than to be different. But I now realized the result of being like everyone else would be an inability to create, since my creativity was forged entirely from darkness and pain, not light and joy. And the gift of conceiving something from nothing was as close to ecstasy as I would ever get—an absolute sense of freedom in giving form to white space and bringing it to life. That was my control over discord and the feeling I craved more than any other. Since creating, giving, sharing and connecting gave me reasons to get out of bed each morning and defined why I was here, it was imperative to embrace the onerous qualities fostering my ability to do so. For if I could channel my introversion, introspection, despondency, agitation, and questioning into positivity linking me to others, then my life would have meaning and my existence make sense. My salvation was birthed directly from my curse.

In order to derive purpose, my abiding mission was now to *channel darkness into light and forge meaning through connecting with others.* Creating was my most compelling reason to live and armor against meaning-lessness, though continuing to do so every day of my life would be an all-consuming battle. The intention to never stop transforming pain into positivity had to be resolute and my actions deliberate or I would succumb. It was imperative to push forward and continually create one product after another, disallowing my brain to question the purpose of my efforts and convince

me they were futile—
wresting meaning from
the meaninglessness
of existence and order
from chaos. If I didn't
make continual creation
a practiced pattern and
unwavering commitment
I would promptly
be overtaken by the
reality of existence and
drown. And if I could
keep acting and not
thinking it would be the
definition of courage
and path to heal and
make me whole. I always
repeated my favorite
Gertrude Stein quote in
times of desperation, as
it was so appropriate to
my condition: *"We all
fear death and question
our place in the universe.
The artist's job is not to
succumb to despair, but to
find an antidote for the
emptiness of existence."*
That antidote for me,
of course, was creation
itself—continual and
incessant creation.

"*We all fear death and question our place in the universe. The artist's job is not to succumb to despair, but to find an antidote for the emptiness of existence.*"

GERTRUDE STEIN

I've a very special secret
Imperceptible to see
With the power to turn white space
Into creativity
Breathing life into conception
Shaping art to stand alone
Brings a vital sense of purpose
And a joy I've never known

———

A consciousness of pain
And its affliction to our being
Has the terrors of the world
Torment keen eyes inclined to seeing
The charade of mere existence
With no comfort of repression
Till we channel that despair
Into delight through bold expression

There's no feeling any greater
Than to live as a creator
Birthing animated art
From the bliss within my heart

—

I'm imprisoned in my head
Overwhelmed by constant dread
Serving time inside a room
Forged with bars of utter doom
I'm so desperate to break free
Of the shackles binding me
And be guided by a heart
Pumping effervescent art

Step on out of the head
Moving into the heart
Free to channel all dread
Into jubilant art

———

I must purge the desperate contents
Of my heavy head and heart
And transform disconsolation
Into captivating art

———

I've transposed the noise
To a chorus of toys
In allowing my brain
To wrest joy from this pain

I'm in reverence of a place
Fondly known as pure white space
Rife with possibility
To frame what my mind can see

———

I needn't travel far to find
The vast expanses of my mind
Where solace reigns and thoughts run free
Awash in possibility

———

I leave the blare behind
Navigating through my mind
Resting where all promise flows
Flush with freedom to compose

The products I created
Were designed for others' eyes
Since the need for validation
Made it all about the prize
Then discovered innovation
Was an antidote for me
In unearthing a deep channel
To express authentically

———

Invention's born from conscious space
And not the more cerebral place
So strive to live each day aware
And artistry will flow from there

———

Pure genius versus diligence
Are not at all the same
For despite our ardent efforts
Brilliance cannot be an aim

Hold on tight to your conceptions
In the manner they arise
So they never lose their essence
Once appraised through others' eyes

———

We've a latent spark quite desperate
To manifest its flame
Though for years remains sequestered
Under pretense, fear and shame
Till it cannot be repressed
From raging freely any longer
And must boldly greet the world
To stir a bonfire even stronger

———

Never strive to be creative
Just intent in all you do
As awareness grants the channel
For creation to flow through

When I'm reveling in wonder
I abandon fear and time
Shifting notion to invention
And phonetics into rhyme

———

There would be no innovation
Or bold creativity
If we didn't cherish failure
And embrace uncertainty

———

Let's abandon our depression
Living freely in the soul
Where authentic self-expression
Is our all-abiding goal

The sentence I am serving
For true freedom to create
Is a lifetime spent imprisoned
In this melancholy state

———

My voice flows through my fingertips
In notes, toys, prose and rhyme
Simply channeling affliction
Into artistry sublime

Who would think such desperation
Born of unrelenting grief
Could be funneled to creation
Granting promise and relief

———

This overwhelming sorrow
Also carries heartfelt joy
When purged into deeper meaning
Through each simple verse or toy

———

Directing this internal strife
By all accounts transformed my life
From heartache finding no release
To playthings forging lasting peace

Channel anguish
Into action
Liberated
From distraction
Living fully
In the heart
At whim to forge
Uplifting art

—

If only I existed
In my heart and not my head
I'd be guided by creation
Not this ever-present dread

When my final days draw closer
Prompting reason to reflect
On what brought my life true meaning
And the dots to all connect
It will center on creation
Moving darkness into light
To guide others on the journey
From despair to futures bright

———

It was only when I learned
How to release what was suppressed
That I truly birthed creation
And organically expressed

———

We must take those special gifts
Conceived inside us from the start
And release them to touch others
Bringing solace to the heart

Proudly boasting
To our friends
That we were quite
Intoxicated
Isn't speaking
Of bliss born
From art innately
Generated
But imbibing
Foreign substances
To reach
Inebriation
When creatives
Get their highs
Indulging
Pure imagination

We can't measure in advance
If a new product will succeed
For consumers aren't able
To imagine what they need
And each innovative kernel
Must be delicately sowed
Never certain which will sprout
When benefaction is bestowed

———

All these verses covet freedom
And the tunes desire light
Though I'm bound to live grief-stricken
Knowing most will lose the fight

———

I will live completely free
When my truth authentically
Wholly channels into art
From the candor in my heart

I'll use this pain
For others' gain
Transforming how I feel
Into light within
So kids begin
To play and help me heal

———

Invention may spring forward
From a chasm of white space
Conjured deep within the stretches
Of that enigmatic place
Or lie shrouded from existence
In a block of wood or stone
Till it's chipped away to brandish
A true masterpiece unknown

———

My only path to peace
Is to let all wanting cease
With clear head and open heart
Shaping scintillating art

A masterpiece may surface
Out of nothing but thin air
Or have risen long ago
Then cast aside to languish there
Till it's once again awakened
By a soul that hears its cry
And restores that timeworn essence
To emerge a butterfly

—

One can't fashion brilliant artwork
Without owning a deep sense
Of the wonder that surrounds them
Rousing passion so intense
It demands to be expressed
Through music, painting, rhyme or prose
Forging glimmers of amazement
Into rapturous repose

I was born a helpless victim
Filled with terror from the start
Yet found lasting hope and purpose
Through expression from the heart

———

I must channel pain to product
Or I'll suffocate in woe
For the grief is all but killing me
With nowhere else to go

———

We depend on the deep insight
Of a bold, impassioned few
To forge music, art and poetry
And etiquette eschew
Yet they're labeled as eccentric
And maligned for being weird
When those birthing timeless treasures
Are ordained to be revered

If I harness the depression
Turning anguish to expression
And foreboding into light
It will validate the fight

———

This magic that's within us
Is the source of our salvation
For it alters deep despair
Into transformative creation

———

Do you dream up the ideas
Or conceive between the lines
For true classics take bold vision
Fused with masterful designs

Don't just be a dancer
Feel the rhythm in each move
Don't just be a singer
Find the pulse within the groove
Don't just be a writer
Flow as freely as the words
Don't just be a pilot
Soar euphoric as the birds
Don't just be a painter
Merge completely into art
Don't just be a thinker
Live unbridled in the heart

———

All these decades orchestrating
This impassioned symphony
Weaving overwhelming joy
With waves of abject misery
Forge the tale of my existence
Ringing powerful and true
And beseeching liberation
So the world can hear it too

We can follow pure convention
Apprehended by routine
Or delight in every nuance
Birthing concepts never seen

———

When we tackle novel ventures
Without knowing all the rules
We employ our intuition
Not the antiquated tools

———

I cannot live constrained
By others' formulaic rules
For without inventive thinking
We are simply brainwashed fools

I have found the only purpose
Of their systems, codes and rules
Is to break them and soar free
Armed with a novel set of tools

———

Some believe that formal process
Will facilitate success
But it only serves to stifle
True creative boundlessness

Every symphony is waiting
Within scads of random notes
Every novel circulating
Through disjointed words and quotes
Every sculpture is lamenting
Under dull, amorphous stone
Landscapes seamlessly inventing
From a wash of varied tone
Every unexpressed creation
Living shrouded from the light
Till awarded liberation
From a soul that grants its flight

———

This compulsion to create
Is immeasurably great
For I need to know the pain
Hasn't ravaged me in vain

It's the *learning*, not the grade
It's the crafting, not what's *made*
It's *crusading*, not the war
It's competing, not the *score*
It's the *acting*, not the part
It's the painting, not the *art*
It's the *journey*, not the goal
For the process fuels the *soul*

——

I have never contemplated
Innovations here tomorrow
Just transforming present sorrow
Into pleasure unabated
Proudly living decades later
Motivated by the passion
Shaping every piece I fashion
Now a genuine creator

Wouldn't it be wonderful
If what has salvaged me
Could help others find the strength as well
To live contentedly

———

A great novel isn't written
Without drafts strewn on the floor
Or a landscape formulated
Without splattered paint before
A skyscraper isn't framed
Without a host of sketched designs
Or concerto orchestrated
Without iterated lines
For creating works of art
Requires countless grueling tries
And continual refinement
For true classics to arise

If I simply let creation
Flow unbridled from my heart
Unaware of who it touches
Or what feeling will impart
I'll experience a freedom
That I've never truly known
With the power to turn anguish
Into music all my own

———

Creatives are maligned
For being overly dramatic
Exceedingly despairing
And uncommonly dogmatic
When it's those divergent qualities
That birth such brilliant art
And we all deserve a chance
To be exalted from the start

CREATIVITY—*Words*

This wasn't poetry requiring higher-level thought processes to decipher, but just a simplified translation of my deepest fears, insights and unanswered questions to make sense of them in digestible form.

Although the majority of my everyday thoughts were existential in nature—dark, despairing and too complex to ever be formally answered or even adequately discussed—the manner by which I intellectualized them through written verse came out innocent and straightforward. As I matured to read the words of real poets, I was ashamed with writing so simply and my reflections emerging plainly as a child's. This wasn't poetry requiring higher-level thought processes to decipher, but just a simplified translation of my deepest fears, insights and unanswered questions to make sense of them in digestible form. And since they had already been pondered and reduced to their essence, no one would ever view them as more profound. Yet although I knew these writings would never be dissected intellectually, I still somehow believed they had power to touch others grappling with similar concerns.

The first legitimate opportunity to liberate my verses came after Doug and I discovered the sole manufacturer of our company's wooden puzzles had betrayed us by copying and bringing our very designs to market. This deceit left us so morally outraged we decided to abandon the toy business altogether and apply to graduate school. I would follow my dream of becoming a writer and earn an MFA in Creative Writing (poetry), while Doug would embark on the path to becoming a university President. We chose to apply to only one institution, the University of Connecticut, as it was right in our backyard and the most affordable option.

And I soon learned my application required submission
of a selection of writing, an opportunity that made
me nervous, but also incredibly hopeful. I had never
before exposed these words, and was eager to be seen
as having potential to become *(in my wildest dreams,
of course)* an Emily Dickinson or Robert Frost, my two
poetry idols.

Given I was applying to an establishment with an
unranked writing program, I never imagined the
response from the department head would be so
contrary to the fairy tale ending I envisioned. For I was
soundly rejected from the program, and his critique
of my submissions was brutally scathing. *"Your poetry
is truly* SOPHOMORIC," he concluded, *"and clearly
not of the caliber our program demands."* Now the
Merriam-Webster definition of sophomoric is *"lacking
in maturity, taste or judgment."* And the first few
thesaurus.com words emerging when typing
sophomoric are IDIOTIC, FOOLISH, ABSURD,
STUPID, HALF-WITTED, AND SILLY. So needless
to say, I was left reeling from the cruelty of that one
word assessing my life's most meaningful work. For
rejecting my poetry was rejecting the very essence
of who I was, since the words poured out of me as
they were, albeit simple. They were the way I made
sense of convoluted feelings, questions and ideas,
and to overcomplicate would render them unable to
be effectively processed or understood. Moreover, to
be told they were *"stupid"* at an institution not even

selective about whom they accepted into their mediocre program was the ultimate slap in the face. In fact, I vowed to never again let my "*poetry*" see the light of day—now certain it would never be appreciated. Thank goodness we chose to forge ahead with our business and not pursue graduate education, but I was so profoundly impacted by that rejection that I completely ceased writing for the subsequent two and a half decades. And although I continued channeling that creative energy into designing thousands of toys during the same period, I still remain devastated to have let the opinion of one person stifle my voice and dramatically impact my life.

The poetry rejection reemphasized I was a misfit in a world moving to an entirely different beat. I saw myself as the little child in the story *"The Emperor's New Clothes,"* who exclaimed, *"The emperor isn't actually wearing any clothes!"* and thinking all the while, *"Why can't these older and wiser individuals see he isn't wearing clothes?"* Since in reflecting back on my education, I never honestly believed any member of my English classes truly understood the poetry they were being asked to analyze. In essence, high school and college classes mirrored *"The Emperor's New Clothes,"* with students pressured to pretend they understood by concocting deep meaning to interpret others' writings, when nearly all of them were thinking…*"I don't have a clue what this person is saying...or even care about deciphering it...or much less enjoy the writing itself!"*

I had a distinct mindset that the sole purpose of art and poetry was to instantly touch the hearts of viewers/ readers—left baffled why sincere feelings were masked in flowery language, colors or costume to become so burdensome individuals needed semester-long courses and advanced degrees to decipher their meaning. I knew the answer had to be one of two reasons, or perhaps even a combination of both: 1) the artist/poet felt the need to overcomplicate their work to appear *"more learned"* than it was and appeal to intellectuals, and 2) the intellectuals themselves felt the need to overcomplicate, read into or see more in creations than existed to validate their advanced degrees. I always wished these learned professors and students would be granted the privilege of speaking with creators themselves to ask if this implicit meaning was indeed hidden within the text/creation. Because I knew a majority of creators would simply laugh out loud and say *"obviously not...you've just contrived it to fill your need for intellectual validation,"* confirming my hypothesis that such manufactured complexity was largely egoic. But the tragic result of having either the creator, decipherer or both overcomplicating their message/analysis was that the majority of artistic works appealed to many fewer people than they should have, remaining in the head and not felt by the soul. I never understood or enjoyed the majority of scholarly poetry I read throughout life, falling in love with the simplest poems of Emily Dickinson and Robert Frost since their plainly conveyed messages resonated so deeply

*If the majority
of audiences
couldn't readily
derive meaning
and joy
from one's creation,
then what purpose
did it serve?*

with my heart. Poetry shrouded in complexity and
requiring intense analysis over extended periods was
counterintuitive, since art should arouse powerful
feelings in the heart and not become cerebral exercises
reserved for intellectuals. Staying in our heads actually
prevented us from feeling with our hearts, when the
magic of art was to simply connect with others and
evoke genuine emotion!

If the majority of audiences couldn't readily derive
meaning and joy from one's creation, then what
purpose did it serve? But maybe I was once again
thinking too naively, although surely if I felt this
way others *must* also feel similarly. Because most of
us didn't have advanced degrees in English and Art
History, and no wherewithal to understand artistry that
should immediately captivate our hearts. I believed all
energies should be focused, in the instance of a poem,
on drawing powerful connections with its ability to
interpret deep questions and fears, and with a product
on engaging instantly and having an intensely impactful
experience. To be honest, I always felt *"sophomoric"*
myself when it came to advanced works of art or
literature and ashamed I didn't *"understand them
intellectually,"* yearning to have them tug on my heart-
strings. For surely the intent of creators was to kindle
genuine emotion. And yet, perhaps my frustration
was just pure rationalization for the fact that I wrote
continual *"poetry,"* but it was nothing like the words of
studied poets and more like greeting card messages

or song lyrics. But unfortunately even if I wanted the verses to sound more scholarly I had no choice, as those were what gushed out of me and I transcribed them exactly as they appeared in my head. Yet they were counter to what everyone believed poetry should be, since those writing and reading poetry were highly cultured and saw themselves as true scholars. In essence, embracing my poetry would be acknowledging they were simple and not erudite, which would be frowned upon by their learned peers.

The most miraculous occurrence of my life, however, was when this mindset regarding the intention of art and poetry became the philosophy I used in creating toys. My favorite toy design mantra became *"low skill, high impact,"* since as with poetry most toys were overcomplicated and difficult to simply enjoy. The basic skills they purported to teach were completely lost in contrived bells, whistles and intricacy masking their true essence and ultimately hampering a child's engagement. I created toys entirely differently than other toymakers— focusing on timeless play patterns, themes and skills, but reinventing them through appealing, realistic features and functional pizzazz, enhanced play value, ease of use and assembly, and engaging graphics (along with superior quality and accessible pricing). I passionately believed playing with a toy shouldn't require a manual and high degree of intellect, but instead immediately captivate and stimulate a child's senses. Even our more sophisticated games and crafts were designed to be easily

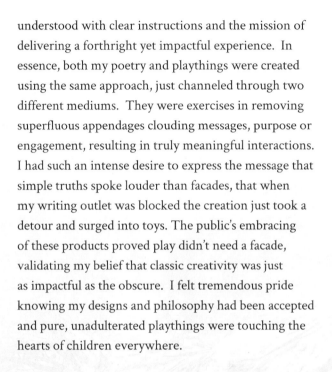

understood with clear instructions and the mission of delivering a forthright yet impactful experience. In essence, both my poetry and playthings were created using the same approach, just channeled through two different mediums. They were exercises in removing superfluous appendages clouding messages, purpose or engagement, resulting in truly meaningful interactions. I had such an intense desire to express the message that simple truths spoke louder than facades, that when my writing outlet was blocked the creation just took a detour and surged into toys. The public's embracing of these products proved play didn't need a facade, validating my belief that classic creativity was just as impactful as the obscure. I felt tremendous pride knowing my designs and philosophy had been accepted and pure, unadulterated playthings were touching the hearts of children everywhere.

It was beneficial that our toys, unlike my poetry, had children playing with them as evaluators versus a scholarly, university professor who wasn't the target audience. In fact, the evaluating audience was another critical distinction between elusive "*art*" and our playthings, in that we depended on those actively using products to provide feedback and never sought approval of those critiquing from above. Hence we rarely submitted our toys for industry awards and never won "*coveted gold seals,*" since those awards generally weren't determined by actual parents or children but based on financially supporting the award organizations themselves. That made them irrelevant to us. The only *"awards"* we sought were accolades coming from legitimate consumers: teachers, parents, caregivers and children engaging with products firsthand. No one else's opinion served the genuine mission of enthralling children and unleashing their imaginations through open-ended play.

When the floodgates could no longer dam my repressed feelings and I began writing decades later, I became adamant about never calling my verses *"poetry"* again, as I now knew the name poetry would be misleading in overstating what I wrote. Poetry still implied that an intellectual with advanced degree needed to elevate it above regular people to plainly experience. I wanted to move as far away from that definition as possible, since what emerged from me was simple and direct. So perhaps I just needed to change what these verses were called, not the words themselves, for the name I could change, the words I could not. And maybe, just maybe, that would enable my writings to be accepted. Because for good or for bad, I still had an acute need for these words to be embraced, since they were the truest expressions of my soul and had been unwavering beacons over my lifetime. Yet they were tragically gathering dust in the shadows, clamoring to connect with others as I was desperately trying to do with my own heart. So I pondered what they truly meant to me. Names like

SIMPLIFICATIONS, EXPRESSIONS, REALIZATIONS, REFLECTIONS
and RUMINATIONS surfaced, but didn't eloquently convey
their magnitude. Or merely the word *"verses,"* which I
had been using as a generic, but wasn't nearly evocative
enough. However, I was strolling along a favorite beach
with Doug brainstorming names when it hit me like
a lightning bolt: *Life*Lines. I am obsessed with double
meanings, and this was the ultimate since those words
were indeed *Life*Lines in both their format and intent.
Today, they are no longer my poems but my *Life*Lines,
representing a five decade manifesto of my deepest
fears, questions and insights translated into mantras
keeping me safe and sane.

Having now reframed what these writings are called I
am much more apt to share them. For in reality, I never
intended for them to be analyzed but simply *felt* in
potentially capturing a revelation, thought, question,
or sentiment someone else had also experienced, but
was unable to articulate. And having been steadfast
comrades throughout every turbulent life storm, I
hoped they could provide a source of comfort to others
needing *Life*Lines as well.

In allowing these words to flow through me once
again I could finally submit to the awe arising from
wholeheartedly embracing them—entirely intoxicated
by their sounds. Combinations of certain syllables were
so pleasurable I would develop goosebumps while

I was stunned to see
these words hadn't
been willing to
remain repressed in
perpetuity—ultimately
dredging a tunnel from
my heart out my arm
then fingers to proclaim
my authentic voice.

enunciating them—rolling off my tongue and suffusing me in pure solace. Vicissitudes, revelatory, omnipotent, soliloquy, magnificent, epiphany, mellifluous, luminescent, preposterous, breathtaking, perseverate, ephemeral and fervor were just a handful of shiver-inducing favorites. And although I had imprisoned them for decades, I now knew rhyming words sang my fundamental life song—in organically uniting they had a rhythm and tune uniquely mine yet entirely their own. I knew these basic words, more than any other medium—so plain and seemingly uninspiring individually with their jumbled combinations of letters deemed irrelevant by most—forged such a powerful message when streaming from my hand and synthesizing in rhyme. They so poignantly transcribed what flowed through my being, were my internal life script, and I was desperate to hear these mantras, which had become my indispensable *Life*Lines, run off the lips and play in the heads and hearts of others. Words had always been my innate method of expression, just channeled through my hand rather than from my lips for fear of ridicule and rejection in using my actual voice. Yet although I had silenced them for years, I was stunned to see these words hadn't been willing to remain repressed in perpetuity—ultimately dredging a tunnel from my heart out my arm then fingers to proclaim my authentic voice. And in actuality, I spoke much more honestly through my fingers than ever from my mouth.

I now saw each and every word imbued with breath, heartbeat and unique voice playing pure, unfiltered music and the song of my soul. The rhythm of words uniting on paper was truly intoxicating, and I would instinctively recite a new verse while drumming on my knee, longing for it to undulate in perfect timing. For when words didn't effortlessly cascade, it represented my inner discord and terrifying sense of powerlessness toward existence, and I was inherently impelled to create harmonious melody and order from that chaos to feel calm amidst the raging storm within. A choppy and off-key verse was like a large pebble in my shoe or a splinter in my finger, throbbing and demanding extrication until the disparate syllables orchestrated. There was nothing I desired more than freedom from my internal oppression, and the channel to liberation came in morphing senselessness into tangible creation that "*made sense.*"

Transforming despair into positivity through toys had provided a powerful life force no doubt, forging concrete meaning and enabling me, though indirectly, to touch others and impact their lives. It had done a noble job in serving me well for three decades and I was eternally grateful. However, given this newfound understanding of who I was and acceptance of my eccentricities and hypersensitivities, my soul was seeking more. For funneling pain into appealing content for the world to embrace was actually the same pattern I had engaged in my entire life by masking my

There was nothing
I desired more than
freedom from my
internal oppression,
and the channel
to liberation came
in morphing
senselessness into
tangible creation that
"made sense."

*They were the air
I breathed, the first
image I saw when I
awoke each morning
and the last vision
running through my
head as I fell asleep
each night.*

true self in a pretty package to appear someone
else. And it was indeed my words and words alone
reflecting my core essence. Yet those words were not
wrapped in a beautifully designed package with big
logo and eye-catching graphics; they were every bit
as unsettled and yearning as my soul—sometimes
reveling in wonder, sometimes despairing, sometimes
questioning and other times angry and demanding
answers. And they always emerged authentically with
nothing obscuring their truth or complicating their
meaning. They had never let me down, were my truest
and often only friends, and had humbly become my
most cherished teachers. They were so much wiser and
more profound than I, and I trusted them more than
anyone or anything as they brought such comfort, joy
and guidance that I would instantly perish without
their sustenance. They were the air I breathed, the first
image I saw when I awoke each morning and the last
vision running through my head as I fell asleep each
night. They played the song of my life, keeping me
alive all these years through every single heartache and
hurdle. And I was desperate to have them uplift others
as they had uplifted me.

I had kept these words hidden in the shadows much too
long—my entire life, actually, petrified they would be
rebuffed as they had by that English professor nearly
30 years earlier. Their rejection had been one of the
greatest tragedies of my life, as I let its shame shackle
them in silence when I knew they deserved so much

more. For these *Life*Lines were as living, breathing
and vibrant as I, and clamoring to light up the world
through sparking minds, rolling off tongues and
touching souls with heartfelt aphorisms. And in wholly
embracing their significance I realized they not only
carried despair as I originally believed, but beauty,
wonder and hope as well. They just plainly reflected
the many divergent sides of Melissa—I was darkness
and I was light, not to mention rage, doubt, awe and
curiosity as well. For three decades I had channeled
desolation into light through birthing toys, believing
I must hide every bit of innate despair from the world.
But in hiding that anguish I was still masking the
essence and duality of who I truly was, since my light
only emanated from my darkness. Hence now, crossing
into this sixth decade of existence, I needed to accept
life and myself as a combination of joy and pain *plus*
darkness and light, catalyzing to forge my entirety of
being and all creation surging forth from within.

My words stand proudly unadorned
Souls bared for all to see
Never hopelessly enshrouded
In contrived obscurity
Tempted not by pomp or pretense
No intention to confound
Humbly voice no lesser essence
Through simplicity of sound

———

These words forge a raging river
Coursing madly through my head
With a fervent need to unify
And dam the endless dread
Bravely serving as clear beacons
In each contemplative verse
They will ever be my lifelines
Though torment me like a curse

I am straddling the line
Between pure mania and bliss
For at times the words bear anguish
And at others hold promise
When they channel freely through me
I soar higher than a kite
But ensnared in my subconscious
Coldly menace day and night

———

Will there ever come a day
When all these rhymes relent their flow
With no questions left to ask
Or incongruities to show?
When rejoicing in the moment
Offers everything I need
Living blissfully contented
And conceptually freed?

Keep it coming
Bring it on
Attack me with your wrath
For I no longer
Feel the blows
As I have found my path
And all the years
I lost so wholly
Shackled by your chains
Behind me now
With grief transformed
To verse pumped through my veins

These ever streaming verses
Surging madly through my head
Are clamoring relentlessly
To make sense of the dread
Are fighting to find reason
To endure despite the pain
And demanding liberation
From this overactive brain

———

I am holding them all hostage
Frantic prisoners in my head
Endless words that beg for freedom
And permission to be read
Fearful if I hold them captive
And restrain them from the light
They will never know true meaning
Doomed to end their futile fight

There is nothing
More sublime
Than when words
Commune in rhyme
A syllabic
Symphony
Playing
Poignant poetry

———

Some words hurt, deceive and punish
Mine just comfort and sustain
Ever loyal, trusted comrades
In this war to banish pain
And it's only by their side
I've found an everlasting way
To move darkness into light
And live to face another day

When these humble words find meaning
Freely mingling in rhyme
I am overcome by rapture
Absent worries, fear or time
For to take this utter madness
Ever streaming through my head
And transpose it into verses
Making sense of all the dread
Leaves me certain there's a light
Within the caverns of my soul
And believe there must be reason
To persist despite the toll

———

All these words that vent through rhyming
Will not lift me past the mind
Till they coincide in timing
With the truth I seek to find

My voice rarely leaves these lips
But boldly channels through my hand
For I find most discourse challenging
Since answers can't be planned
Often uttering opinions
Which are terribly received
And encountering reactions
So much worse than I perceived
Thereby heading to my corner
Armed with paper and a pen
To release the desolation
Using written words again

———

I fashion simple poetry
To navigate life's lunacy
As folly shifts to form
Quelling tumult from mind's storm

Whenever words run off my lips
They never come out right
With their meaning misinterpreted
And taken as a slight
Overwhelming me in misery
Convinced it made no sense
What cascaded freely from my heart
Was judged as an offense
Hence today I'm apt to share my truths
In verse pumped through my hand
Since most face-to-face relationships
I'm unfit to withstand

———

When discordant words assemble
And resound in harmony
I'm uplifted to a vastness
Far beyond reality
A land rife with optimism
Where despair transforms to song
Now I'm terrified to plummet
Back to where I don't belong

They say focus on your breathing
I must revel in the rhyme
For whenever words unite in song
I lose all sense of time
And in guiding errant syllables
To congregate and flow
I'm expelling desperation
Bringing solace few can know

———

I express in simple words
What conversation can't convey
To relieve disconsolation
And survive another day

———

To find my verses ringing true
In others' heads and ears
Gives me strength to carry on
Despite these unrelenting fears

Words channel through these fingertips
But seldom leave my tongue
For most discourse fades once off the lips
And notes expire once sung
Yet transcribing verse to paper
Yields a memoir on each sheet
To immortalize life's struggles
And quell destiny's drumbeat

———

I deserve to own the podium
At liberty to speak
And articulate opinions
With no burden of critique
I'm not seeking consultation
Or my message modified
Just the fortitude to utter
True expression long denied

Though these simple words emerge
From deep within my shattered soul
When they synthesize in rhyme
The cracks are filled to make me whole

—

I analyze in verse
The fears I strive
To comprehend
Granting fortitude
To battle through
Despair I must transcend

—

Rhyming words are my religion
With each verse a simple prayer
Lending hope and inspiration
Through a lifetime of despair

The people in my universe
Were never round for long
Since I didn't put much faith in those
Who always did me wrong
Leaving words my steadfast comrades
Lending solace through the years
Humbly serving as the forum
To make meaning of my fears

———

I am hopeful countless mantras
Ever ringing in my head
Will bring solace to the hearts
Of others wallowing in dread

I long to make music
From fusions of words
Soulful tunes meant to charm
An ensemble of birds
Soulful tunes meant to ring
Like rich bells in the ears
Soulful tunes meant to carry
Both laughter and tears
Soulful tunes meant to lie
Like fine wine on the tongue
Soulful tunes meant to savor
Years after they've rung

———

My words have been staunch lifelines
Sounding solace through the years
Ably voicing desperation
Chanting hope despite deep fears
When I lost the will to live
They forged a mantra to stand strong
And it's venting by their side
I found the strength to carry on

My words are an arrangement
For the eyes to plainly see
A rich optic celebration
Of a diphthong symphony

———

I have a voice
Quite rarely heard
Yet boldly speaks
Through written word

———

My words are notes
To charm the ear
Yet also beg
The eyes to hear

———

My words congregate in mourning
To transcribe a haunting song
That laments with every breath I take
And will my whole life long

Writing inundates the heart
While poet subjugates the head
And we must indulge the soul
Or ego will prevail instead

———

I yearn to take these terrors
Far too vast to comprehend
And transform them into meaning
Through the simple words I've penned

———

These rhymes must be embodied
To breathe freely on their own
And decipher life's enigmas
In their plainly stated tone

When these agitated words
Race unrestrained inside my head
I just buff their unhewn edges
So they harmonize instead

—

This story must be told
For these words cannot grow cold
And must rise to meet the gaze
Of those drowning in malaise

Why shouldn't it be my words
Ringing true in someone's ears?
Why shouldn't it be my words
Helping others face their fears?
Why shouldn't it be my words
Forging empathy and hope?
Why shouldn't it be my words
Lending strength and will to cope?
Why shouldn't it be my words
Guiding seekers on their way
When these words are every reason
I'm still standing here today

Words comprise my very essence
Who I am and what I'll be
And my life will lack true meaning
Till they find affinity

———

Words have offered me a lifeline
And compassion when in need
Yet will only prompt salvation
Once their messages are freed

———

Words express my deepest yearnings
And exactly how I feel
Yet will only render meaning
Giving others strength to heal

If the mind is closed to learning
Words will never touch the heart
As they seek a soul that's yearning
For their wisdom to impart

———

I fashion simple poetry
To contemplate absurdity
And translate what's inane
Into verse that keeps me sane

———

In most cases words are meaningless
And actions are what matter
But for me these words are everything
And hardly idle chatter
For they represent a road map
Granting requisite direction
Through life's countless twists and turns
Impelled to reach profound connection

To know my words are echoing
In someone else's ears
And affording them good reason
To persist despite their fears
Or just running off the lips
Of folks in ordinary speech
And transmitting a clear message
To ignite real change or teach
Will most surely grant salvation
And help validate the pain
With a vital sense of purpose
This crusade is not in vain

VOLUME TWO

LONELINESS

There is no doubt my greatest life yearning was to gain others' acceptance and bask in the glow of "fitting in and belonging."

There is no doubt my greatest life yearning was to gain others' acceptance and bask in the glow of *"fitting in and belonging."* However, despite the intensity of this desire I never succeeded, as I was continually rejected for being overly reactive, sensitive and just generally *"odd."* Others saw my behavior as excessive and irritating, for it appeared I was being too dramatic and even intentionally acting hysterical as a ploy to attract attention. No one believed this was just the way I had been born and how stimuli impacted me—for I honestly detested attention in general and especially for weakness, horrified to be viewed as melodramatic. But it was impossible to control my organic reactions, as these emotions had minds of their own with boundless depth and volatility. And when others discounted or dismissed my true feelings, it only further reinforced the contention that no one would ever wholly understand or embrace the real me.

I therefore moved through life acutely aware that there was no acceptance for such extreme feelings by the society in which I functioned and the family with whom I lived. I received the message very early on that heightened reactions weren't openly expressed and manifested to the world, as others didn't approve of such excessive intensity and strong response. It was much more preferable functioning quietly and not calling attention to oneself by acting irrational and causing commotion.

Experiencing life so deeply made me feel like a
wounded animal—misunderstood, betrayed and
drowning in despair that no one cared about my fate
or state, yet powerless to divulge my concerns or
chart an alternate course. I thus remained paralyzed,
floundering in torrents of self-pity certain I was a
victim cast aside by society—a meaningless speck
ultimately disappearing into oblivion without anyone
knowing or lamenting its passage. Seeing others so
blissfully happy while churning in misery segregated me
even further, wondering why I had been born facing
backward while the rest of the world moved in the
opposite direction. This malaise never passed yet wasn't
something I could even articulate, just a deep sense that
no one was as strange as I, no one would ever embrace
my peculiarities, and I was utterly alone with no one
willing to hear my cries.

From early on, reactions of others made me absolutely
terrified of exposing my despondency. In fact, I
can only remember three instances when such desire
for connection moved me to seek outside solace. The
first was when I was rejected from my desired sorority
in college, once again grappling with the realization
that I would never find acceptance and forever remain
a social outcast. Experiencing such public rejection
hit so profoundly that I wanted to transfer schools
immediately, yet couldn't realistically do so and
was left reeling over being deemed a total loser. I
tried conveying the depths of my despair to my then

Seeing others so blissfully happy while churning in misery segregated me even further, wondering why I had been born facing backward while the rest of the world moved in the opposite direction.

boyfriend, explaining I was unable to go on in the face of such renunciation. However he saw me as invincible and effortlessly able to surmount any challenge, attempting to comfort me by making light of the rejection. He admonished: *"Don't even dignify those girls and their stupid sorority—ignore them. You're going to be just fine."* And while that certainly made sense on a superficial level, the truth was this time was different. I wasn't just going to *"get over it and move on,"* having fallen into a dark hole and needing him to embrace the depths of my despair. Yet although I longed for more than perfunctory encouragement, he ultimately didn't want to see or believe the malaise wasn't temporary and fathom the extent of my desperation, even though I begged for his support. The only unfortunate advice he gave was to mask the pain by channeling it into more performance-based activities, which ultimately became my undoing. He insisted, *"Focus on excelling in academics and clubs—remember **that's** why you came to college."* And since I knew no better, I heeded his advice. Instead of actually dissecting my acute feelings of mistrust, failure and betrayal I completely submerged the grief, funneling all effort into academic and extra-curricular performance that subsequent semester, which would be fall of my junior year.

The second time I shared my anguish was after that very junior year, when I coupled my social implosion with an equally punishing academic collapse as well. Academic

performance had always been my greatest strength—my
go-to for validation in consistently achieving excellence
and separating myself from the masses. And I had
actually taken my boyfriend's advice, diving headfirst
into coursework and clubs to begin the year which
provided a welcome distraction from my overwhelming
sense of abandonment. Yet as the semester progressed
with workload and stress mounting, the combination of
over-extension and pressure to perform became so great
I was unable to complete a semester-long term paper,
needing to request an incomplete from my professor
before heading home on winter break.

This academic "*failure*" was the ultimate message that
I would never achieve perfection in anything—signifying I was a complete failure in life, entirely worthless,
and such a devastating blow that I crumpled under its
weight. For it turned out never failing academically had
only become a curse with my inability to handle defeat
when it inevitably occurred. In essence, the expectation
I would continue succeeding on the next assignment or
test had become so great it came to define my existence,
submerging me while the dam repressing every fear
gave way and terror flooded through me unrestrained.
My entire body shook like a leaf, I couldn't utter a
word without stammering and was terrified to even
move—literally paralyzed with certainty disaster was
imminent. My worst fears had become reality, with the
futility of life suffusing my body and leaving me unable
to suppress despair any longer.

I didn't want to suffer such excruciating pain another minute and planned my exit with meticulous detail.

I didn't want to suffer such excruciating pain another minute and planned my exit with meticulous detail. I knew the exact combination of pills it would take to stop my heart, keeping that cocktail in a small prescription bottle tucked deep inside my jeans pocket for when I was ready. My parents happened to be on an extended overseas vacation during that winter break, and I returned home despondent and desperately craving human connection, for my consumption with mortality and self-protection rendered me unable to be left alone, leave the house, or engage in activity for fear I'd critically injure or fatally harm myself in an accident. I was petrified to drive fearing I would crash the vehicle and perish, and even frightened to get into the shower terrified I would slip and suffer a lethal fall. In fact, I felt such panic and need for affinity I had taken to calling movie theaters for hours each day, listening to loops of film selections and playing times just to hear human voices. However, my need for genuine engagement became so intense I then switched to calling airlines, asking for fictitious flight information to keep operators on the phone making small talk. And yet, I still longed for communion with someone willing to embrace the real me and offer words of encouragement, comfort and sincere kinship.

I wracked my brain thinking of someone I could contact, remembering my friend was also home from college and might lend an empathetic ear. I dialed her number and she answered the phone immediately, as I touched on my experience that semester to gauge her response before revealing more. However, her instant reaction confirmed why I had never exposed myself in the past. "*Wait,*" she exclaimed, "*I cannot even believe what I am hearing. You, Melissa, are depressed? This is absurd and cannot be true—because you're perfect, remember? Things like this don't happen to you! In fact, I never imagined you would experience anything like this—I don't even know what to say since I'm absolutely speechless.*"

Experiencing this stunned response immediately made my worst possible nightmare a reality, utterly horrified for having confided in her. Instead of offering the compassion I sought and letting me know she was standing beside me, she reacted with shock, further alienating me. And even worse, she now saw me as imperfect and flawed. Even in my desperate state that wasn't acceptable, so I jumped into survival mode rambling, "*Well that's why I wanted to call because I did feel that way, but was thankfully able to recover and just thought you should know I'm now completely fine.*" And with that I quickly hung up the phone to *never* speak with her again. Just to reiterate: that was our last phone call ever, and she had been a "*friend*" up until that point. But the shame over my disclosure was just too great to maintain a future relationship, not to mention I surely didn't need friends who only saw me in my facade and not for who I truly was.

This exchange also highlighted the intense humiliation concealed within my darkness. I was petrified of exposing my despondency to others since when I did, their incredulity I felt this way or contention the feelings would soon dissipate on their own impelled me to submerge them and feign composure. Thus no one had the slightest idea of what existential turmoil raged within. In fact, if any of those who had known me back then were to read these words they would never in a million years guess they were describing me, adamantly contending this depiction couldn't be further from the truth. They would argue I was the last person to be depressed—always laughing and joking with fortitude to conquer any obstacle. And that, of course, was because I had deliberately vowed to swallow any emotion and hide all negativity, displeasure and discomfort from the world no matter the cost.

Perhaps the reason I feel utterly compelled to share my experience is because manifesting an image of perfection, and thus being perceived as someone we are not, is the story of many of our lives. My perfect facade convinced others I was completely different from whom I innately was. And until society is willing to accept that: 1) there are multitudes of scared, depressed and isolated individuals among us, 2) most desperate people will never reveal their anguished feelings publicly and will project flawless personas for fear of ridicule and rejection, and 3) until we nurture our children to feel loved and accepted, discover themselves, and proudly express their unique voices to derive purpose and build self-esteem, this epidemic of isolation, anxiety and depression will only grow.

About five years ago I decided to go out on a limb once again and share my anguished verses with another close friend. I still remained incredibly anxious over revealing myself, but felt a strong bond I believed would enable me to divulge deeper feelings. I pulled together roughly 50 somber reflections and handed them over, tingling with anticipation at her forthcoming response. In truth, I hoped she would be awed with my profundity though I had certainly never disclosed the turmoil raging within. But I wondered...*"Would my verses resonate with her? Would someone finally understand what I experienced each day and readily offer compassion and kinship?"*

To my dismay, this friend didn't respond for weeks, and her ultimate response left me dumbfounded. For it was simply, *"You were clearly in a dark place when you wrote those poems and I'm relieved you're no longer there."* And that was it. No questions, thoughts, asking to read additional verses, discuss further, or offer a shoulder to lean on. And of course, having no sense for how unbelievably wrong she actually was, since in reality I was in the throes of that agitated state every single day of my life. And those writings detailed ruminations plaguing me yesterday as well as today. How could she fail to see my despair and the fact I often

I had received the message enough times now to know others weren't able to meet me in my pain, wanting to see me as utterly impervious.

still deliberated taking my life to ease the pain? Yet she was unable to acknowledge my truth, choosing instead to sweep aside the darkness and skirt right past it. In essence she was telling me, *"Since this is too overwhelming I'm just going believe you've moved past that period and life is better now."*

Once again, I was left terribly disappointed with no one willing to see the real me. My friend had made it abundantly clear who she was and what she wanted out of her relationships. Namely, she had no desire to dig deeper and touch darkness, content having cursory interactions never broaching the wall of *"appropriateness,"* although I was imploring her to be a lifeline. Or maybe she just wasn't capable of emotional intimacy. Yet either way it didn't matter since I was getting the short end of the stick with my expectations for more dashed, left bitter for exposing myself and facing rejection. And honestly, I knew our relationship would never be the same. She had shown me the level to which it would go and that was no longer enough. Yet despite my efforts to travel deeper and disclose my truth, I was unable to find a comrade willing to journey with me. I had received the message enough times now to know others weren't able to meet me in my pain, wanting to see me as utterly impervious. Reality had proven people preferred staying superficially *"in the light,"* never touching the depths of desolation but rather assuming I had a temporary illness which would pass and I'd be cured. And if that's what everyone wanted, then that's what they would get, for I would never again expose myself in such a public and humiliating manner.

These experiences highlight why depressed people rarely choose to share their despondency with anyone, even close family members. Firstly, they're ashamed to admit weakness as it signifies they are abnormal. Secondly, they're embarrassed asking for help from those who believe they *"have it all together,"* since their lifelong facade has portrayed them as flawless. And thirdly, they don't wish to burden others with perpetual darkness that doesn't rapidly *"get better"* and just *"go away."* One of the main causal factors of depression is isolation, which by definition means individuals have already separated themselves and lost the ability to honestly connect with or trust anyone in their lives. As my personal interactions illustrated, the very few times I revealed despair rendered me embarrassed, angry and self-critical as others became aghast at the extent of my sorrow, ever destined to avoid it, deny it or ask the question, *"Is it finally over and are you all better?"* No one understood or accepted that this anxious, intense, morose person was actually the real me; if they chose to see my despair, it was simply a temporary condition from which I would soon recover. But this *"please get better"* response made me even more depressed, because it implied something was very wrong with me and I needed to *"fix or change"* my intrinsic nature to be loved!

Most unfortunately, my entire foundation rested on the hope that others would ultimately meet me in darkness and understand my despair. And as I became more truthful and saw my relationships for what they were, I realized those in my life were unwilling to meet me there—whether they couldn't relate to what I was feeling, didn't want to relate to it, or a combination of both. No one would ever acknowledge the truth of who I was and recognize the happy face I wore was really the facade. These revelations pushed me to my lowest of lows, since my sole desire had been to connect with others on a more meaningful level. But in the end no one truly cared or had the capacity to embrace the real me. I was destined to forever remain alone, since the tragic result of hiding my true self from the world and adopting a phony, affected persona was never finding my people.

Isolating myself from human contact made me starved for affection and bereft of feeling protected, cherished and loved. Those closest to me were essentially wounded children who had never experienced belonging themselves, leaving them unable to express warmth and emotion verbally or physically. This made early relationships entirely robotic and awkwardly uncomfortable. Given the inability to display affection, there were never spontaneous emotional gestures from family members conveying warmth—just perfunctory pats on the back. These involved holding the person a few

And no one will ever know how desperately I craved genuine physical closeness as a vulnerable child.

inches away with one hand and patting their back a
few times with the other—keeping them at bay as if
petting a potentially aggressive and unfamiliar animal.
In fact, ever since becoming aware of this patting
habit I continually noticed it in those ill at ease with
themselves and affection. The pats my family gave
me, however insignificant as they seemed at the time,
perfectly illustrated the extent of intimacy throughout
childhood. Hugs, on the one hand, were warm,
protective and overflowing with love—demonstrating
that others wished to keep you safe in their arms, never
letting you go. Hugs made you feel secure, comforted
and brimming with self-worth. Pats, on the other
hand, signified that others were obligated to formalize
acknowledgment intellectually, but didn't wish to
embrace you emotionally with their hearts. Being
pat made me feel unworthy of real affection. And no
one will ever know how desperately I craved genuine
physical closeness as a vulnerable child.

Ultimately, as much as I yearned for human touch in
my dreams, I became repulsed by human contact in
reality. Since life experience had proven others didn't
care and were selfishly using me for personal gain,
I was unable to trust their actions or motives. And
without trust, I didn't want them physically close as
they were purely satisfying carnal urges. I saw flirting
and the mating dance between males and females
as entirely self-serving, animalistic and disgusting,

wanting no part of that repulsive game. Males were
nothing more than lions in the jungle preening and
then beating their chests with grotesque animal
noises to lure females into their lair. And afterward
boasting to every pack member of the conquest; it
was clearly all about bragging rights and not real love
or emotional connection. These brutes didn't care
one bit about engaging on a deep personal level, only
wishing to gratify their beastly desires and then pursue
their next score. And that sickened me. Even when
I eventually engaged in physical contact, I became
a third person observing the situation coldly and
clinically, going through the motions but staying as
emotionally detached as possible. I just couldn't enjoy
actions so crude, primitive and uncivilized when others
didn't genuinely respect me and only wished to satiate
their biological needs.

This cynicism made me see myself as a soulless vessel
for others to claw, batter and ultimately destroy
without thought as to how it was hurting me. My days
were spent fervently pleasing without any sense of
purpose or self to create as few ripples as possible and
satisfy others' needs. And I didn't want to feel futile
emotions inside that empty shell, electing to function
as a robot with no one or thing able to inflict damage.
I couldn't bear thinking or feeling inside that vessel as
the suffering was just too great. Thus at some point I
quietly turned off my emotions. I never understood the
meaning of *"dissociate"* in a clinical sense, but realized

for most of my life I actually stopped being present
inside a body that had become a punching bag for the
outside world to pummel. It habitually nodded yes and
sought to serve, never exhibiting any sign of exhaustion,
discomfort or reaction and mechanically providing what
others demanded, since it no longer possessed thoughts,
feelings or opinions of its own. Dissociating ended
up permeating all relationships and every physical
encounter as well, serving in a perfunctory manner and
checking tasks off a list to remain free of the burden of
guilt. To survive in a world only bringing me pain, I
needed to protect myself from ever feeling vulnerable
again. And if I completely avoided experiencing
disappointment and had no expectations for others'
behavior, then I could never be hurt. Therefore no one
in my cynical view served any purpose, and any effort
put into building relationships was for naught.

Although I had always endured the intellectual
pessimism of knowing *"I'm alone"* in my head, as I aged
and dropped enticements of expectation, hope, and
saw circumstances as they truly were, I was left with
only those truths emerging from my scratched lenses
of childhood. And those beliefs were that no one
cared about me and I was entirely alone in my heart. I
now knew with intense clarity my relatives would never
understand and support me in the way I needed, and
were so incapable of providing sustenance I actually felt
sorry for having that expectation of them. Likewise,
my children weren't destined to shower me with

appreciation, praising my servitude and embracing
me with open arms. And even more importantly, my
children weren't just another one of my achievements
intent on behaving and performing exactly how
I needed for validation. And lastly, my friendships
weren't ever going to travel deeper than the superficial
banter occurring on sporting event sidelines which
sapped my energy without fueling my soul. Clearly
no one would ever hear my cries and show me they
genuinely cared, accepted and valued me for who I
was. Hence all humans were now seen under a cloud
of mistrust, since those misperceptions were all I had
ever known and believed. Granted by this point I
wanted to see people as inconsiderate and cruel, so
every selfish action they took and comment they made
only served to validate my claims and I never looked for
contrary evidence to refute those beliefs. This mindset
ultimately became my scapegoat and protection
against vulnerability; if I already presumed there was
no point in even trying and it was all for naught, I
would successfully protect myself from rejection and
disallow any one or thing to change my mind. And that
presumption invariably motivated my daily behavior,
as I gave exactly what was needed to maintain the status
quo, but swore I would never bare my soul and expose
my true self.

I soon protected my heart to such extent I projected
myself as unemotional and indifferent—often feeling
guilty for acting so callous and wishing I could see

love and its physical connection as beautiful. But my image of love had been dashed. Love was not innocent and pure, but a manufactured tool used to manipulate others. My family members said "*I love you*" and patted my back without heartfelt affection, blind to how love actually felt and building sincere relationships. This certainly wasn't intentional as their emotional wells were dry, but having never experienced true connection they had absolutely no capacity to nurture affinity within the family unit.

Most shockingly, I now saw even my product creations as inauthentic in having been birthed for achievement alone, thereby just another facade masking the real me. Using toys as my cover had been a wonderfully effective conduit for channeling despair into hope with positive creation to share. Yet although I felt profound joy and sense of accomplishment in creating playthings, I was still living with deep emptiness—almost as if there was a gaping hole in my heart. For despite the fact I was sharing a piece of myself with the world in bringing toys to children, these products were bought off shelves and not tied to me personally. And I was now desperate for genuine, direct connections with real people, finally ready to emerge from the shadows and rip off the guise. I had been on this earth for five decades and still never exposed who I truly was—which I now accepted as an intense, passionate, agitated, questioning, soulful being still struggling to find meaning each day. Yet I would never find fulfillment until I stopped pretending and revealed my true self to the world, unable to betray my soul any longer.

If my people were indeed *"out there,"* I would need to open my heart in a way I hadn't done since childhood and risk rejection. That would be a scary place to travel at this point, for believing I was entirely alone came from a very powerful and convenient mind story which provided an effective coping mechanism throughout life; indicting humanity and telling myself there was no point in even trying protected me from rejection. Thus if I never exposed myself I would never feel the sting of rejection and maintain the illusion of control. And yet, what an epiphany to realize my people were waiting for me, although I had historically rejected them in the same manner I had rejected myself. But having finally accepted myself for the odd, dark, churning, heady individual I was, I could appreciate and accept others for being that way as well.

Although I had dropped many erroneous childhood beliefs regarding unworthiness, I was still living with the strongest of them, namely: 1) others were selfish, 2) others would ultimately disappoint/hurt me, 3) I could trust no one and therefore, 4) I was utterly alone. Based on this adverse story repeatedly playing in my head, I instinctively dissociated from genuine feeling, disallowing anyone to enter my world and lower my defenses. Yet I was thoroughly exhausted from

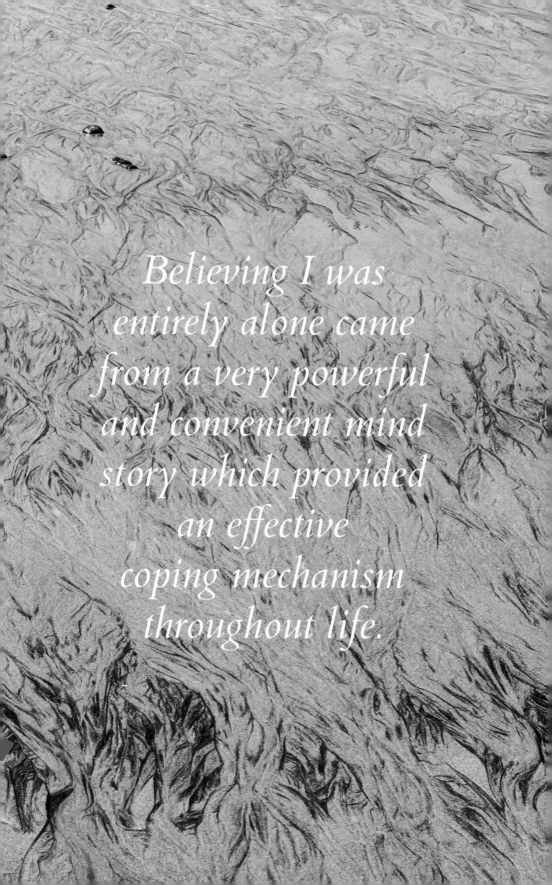

*Believing I was
entirely alone came
from a very powerful
and convenient mind
story which provided
an effective
coping mechanism
throughout life.*

*I would
never find
acceptance
until I
brandished
my truth.*

a lifetime of repression
and resistance, aware
that unless I dramatically
changed my mindset and
opinion of others, I would
never forge meaningful
bonds. This attitude
change extended to family
relationships as well. My
loyal life companion Doug
had been a constant source
of sustenance, although
fear of rejection prevented
me from expressing
my honest feelings or
acknowledging my genuine
needs to him. And I would
never find acceptance
until I brandished my
truth. Yet although
terrified of divulging my
naked soul, there was no
going back and I was finally
ready to plunge into the
turbulent waters of vulnerability to find the love I had
ever been seeking.

If you see yourself as severed
From the world in all its glory
Then you'll distance from accord
And trust mind's fabricated story
That we're different from each other
And will always be alone
When in truth we are the world
With vast potential still unknown

We won't access what is waiting
Past the boundaries we know
Living captive in our heads
And disconnected from life's flow
Till the moment we surrender
To that greater force above
Soaring far beyond seclusion
Undivided in pure love

———

We belong to something larger
Than we ever could have known
Which won't manifest itself to us
Until we've clearly shown
We are open to connection
Far beyond our bounded skin
Since it's only in communion
That transcendence will begin

How I long to find that someone
Who will care enough to see
I am overwrought with anguish
Fear and insecurity
Who will look me in the eye
And know exactly how I feel
Seeing far beyond my lifelong
Inclination to conceal
Who will show me pure compassion
When I'm struggling to cope
Standing firmly in my corner
As a steadfast source of hope
Who will hold me in their arms
And tell me everything's okay
For I'm cherished as I truly am
Not any other way

For years I hid inside myself
A prisoner of the mind
Certain I could not escape these bars
Though willingly confined

———

A whole lifetime of repression
Hasn't eased my deep depression
For I cannot keep on hiding
Fears that sorely need confiding

———

Our propensity to stifle
Builds a wall around our hearts
And entraps us in delusion
Where the path to discord starts

True friendships aren't static
But an undulating flow
Which reflect life's joys and heartaches
Through their every high and low
And though friends may sometimes hurt us
By an unkind act or word
We must manifest compassion
Moving past distress incurred
Since not one of us is perfect
Apt to surely make mistakes
Yet remaining empathetic
Is what building friendship takes

———

If everyone could see
They are essentially the same
Kindred spirits on life's journey
To discover their true aim
Then perhaps they'd show compassion
For their comrades here on earth
Since connection with each other
Is the portal to rebirth

We all clench against existence
Prompted by our deep resistance
To the fears we can't control
Which encapsulate the soul
In seclusion disconnected
With our egos well-protected
From the kinship we so need
To be spiritually freed

———

With my feelings left bereft
Behind a fabricated wall
I was powerless to form
Any authentic bonds at all

The connection we are seeking
Stays eternally denied
When the essence of our being
Waits imprisoned deep inside

———

We exist upon the surface
Living superficially
With the truths we long to broadcast
Shrouded from the world to see

———

It's a shame we hold in custody
Our thoughts and how we feel
When the pathway to belonging
Takes expressing what is real

I'm still racing far and wide
In search of somewhere to call home
A land brimming with potential
And expansiveness to roam
Where delight in being different
Supplants blind conformity
And I swell with heartfelt purpose
Wholly confident in me

———

The times I am the most alone
Are when I'm in a crowd
Finding those with whom I congregate
Appearing to stand proud
And then gradually begin to feel
As if I've shrunk in size
With no fortitude to measure up
In anybody's eyes
Thereby consequently wishing
I had simply stayed as one
For in solitude there's never need
To make comparison

I've been beckoning a lifetime
For a valiant knight on steed
To come prancing in and rescue me
A fairytale indeed
Yet no happily ever after
Comes to fools who wait in vain
Doomed to spend my life alone
With no protection from the pain

———

I have always felt alone
Unjustly labeled an outsider
Since the way I act and think
Could not forge chasms any wider

———

With every spoken word
I move further from the herd
Just a loner unaccepted
Isolated and rejected

Please come meet me in my darkness
Don't just linger in my light
For although I feign this pleasant smile
Most days are dim not bright
I'm not asking for salvation
But imploring you to see
I'm still yearning for acceptance
Of my true entirety

Most folks would rather meet me
In my joy than in my pain
It's much warmer to be standing
In the sunlight than the rain
And far easier to revel
In what's hopeful than what's bleak
Hence I huddle in the shadows
Though my heart so longs to speak

——

Chasing physical perfection
Leaves our honest selves denied
And impedes us from connecting
To what's beautiful inside

We exhaust our days believing
All these troubles are our own
And our fears unique to us
Destined to agonize alone
When in truth we must depend
On our collective empathy
To sustain us through misfortune
And survive adversity

———

I've been summoning my people
Yet they're nowhere to be found
Off sequestered in the darkness
Too repressed to make a sound
Ever fearful trusting others
Will elicit hurt and lies
Hence I venture forward solo
Still alone despite my cries

From what I'm told
I am quite cold
And mask my feelings well
As it's highly rare
I choose to share
And surface from my shell

———

Others thought they knew me well
But surely never would have guessed
That I harbored such resentment
Kept entirely repressed
For my casual demeanor
And free-spirited aplomb
Masked the anguish I endured
Beneath that manufactured calm
While the truth of my existence
Masquerading in facade
Couldn't bear the utter shame
Of being shunned and labeled odd

It's much simpler to blame others
Than acknowledge our misdeeds
Though propensity to vilify
Sows hatred's latent seeds

———

When contempt suffuses being
With the fury it imparts
We dissociate from seeing
Past walls forged between our hearts

———

We must attempt
To rid contempt
From clouding all we see
For imparting hate
Portends our fate
Will end in misery

A real friend dries our tears
Then gets us right back in the game
A real friend shares our grief
With tales of feeling just the same
A real friend shows us mercy
When we openly confide
A real friend never leaves
When we are desperate to hide
A real friend lifts us up
When life is leading us astray
A real friend takes our hand
And always helps us find the way

———

A true friend is that someone
Who despite their own despair
Can still manifest compassion
And convey they truly care

We're each independent rays
Connected to a vibrant sun
And the moment we return back home
Will harmonize as one

———

We are not who we believe
Defined by title, wealth or fame
But creative, loving spirits
All essentially the same

———

We may think we need another
To fulfill and make us whole
Till we make the journey inward
And find concord in our soul

We blame those in the present
For transgressions of the past
Thereby making it a challenge
To forge marriages that last

———

People miles away in distance
May connect right from the start
While some spending years together
Still remain a world apart

We won't teach someone a different truth
By judging what was done
But in showing them a new path
So we all believe we've won

———

We presume we're all so different
But that's clearly not the case
For in truth those so-called oddities
Afflict the human race

155

What isn't ever loved
Cannot be fully understood
And we all deserve the chance
To be adored and seen as good

———

Before you chide
Look deep inside
The ones you so disdain
Intent to see
Them differently
And understand their pain

It's our failure to love others
Just as who they truly are
That engenders all our pain
And keeps us yearning from afar

—

When someone shuts their heart
We may be moved to close our own
But must strive and keep it open
To prevent a life alone

By embracing the perfection
That exists within our hearts
We'll forgive the errors made
By all the ancillary parts

——

It's our flaws that make us human
For perfection just impedes
Us from forging the communion
Our soul desperately needs

——

We are already perfection
But enshrouded in such fear
We've forgotten how to love ourselves
And find our purpose here

We're more similar than different
Yet won't know it to be true
Till we transcend isolation
And affinity shines through

———

Perhaps this desolation
Would just simply cease to be
With the knowledge we're all yearning
To unite in harmony

———

We can manifest that which
The soul has yet to realize
Once we soar above our solitude
As one to harmonize

Thinking someone else will save us
Truly hinders our success
In discovering real purpose
And fomenting happiness

———

It's a shame that you and I
Will never truly know each other
For your essence lies submerged
And masquerading as another
Guided solely by the brain
With no affinity to find
For when ego runs the show
The heart succumbs to selfish mind

There's no sentiment behind
The shallow questions you ask me
Checking boxes off a list
With no respect or empathy
And although you are oblivious
To ever needing more
I still wish you truly saw me
Since pretension I deplore

———

How I wish you had the wherewithal
To see me as I am
For without that this relationship
Is nothing but a sham

If I told you I was drowning
Would you turn the other way
Or dive headfirst in to save me
Apt to rescue or betray?

———

I'm disgusted by these humans
And their narcissistic ways
Which is why I'll be remaining
An outsider through my days

———

To demand esteem from others
Without earning their respect
Leads to fabricated feeling
And what more would you expect?

Though another's words and actions
May offend, hurt and appall
They're oft born from misbeliefs
And never meant for us at all

———

The one with whom I've shared
My inmost questions, hopes and fears
Is recouped by me to do so
And by training lends her ears
To enable me to purge myself
With no remorse or guilt
As there's never obligation
For a deeper friendship built

———

When we listen to another
With wholehearted empathy
We allow them to express the truths
That set their spirit free

If out of
Every crying eye
One tear was shed for me
All this pain
Would surely drift away
Upon the salty sea

———

What does it mean to listen
To another with your heart
It means having no agenda
Or opinion to impart
But embracing them as equals
Granting ample time and space
To receive them in totality
With insight, warmth and grace

I went through life believing
I was utterly alone
Bound to never find connection
Undetected and unknown
Like a negligible cloud
Obscured amidst the hazy sky
And a helpless leaf suspended
Left to fall from limb on high
Just a single wave whose rush
Was stifled by the ocean's roar
And one tiny grain of sand
Lost on the coast's expansive shore
When if only I had quieted
My influential mind
I'd have seen us all as yearning
For acceptance from mankind
And perhaps achieve communion
From that place of empathy
To surmount the separation
And resound in harmony

165

VOLUME THREE

NATURE

168

I never disclosed it to anyone for fear of ridicule,
but from my earliest memories nature spoke to
me—conveying its feelings in distinctly resonant voices.
Nature's cast of characters engaged in relationships
seeming human, and I reflected on them with pure
reverence: the oak tree whispered and told me how
sad it felt as its leaves were falling to the ground, the
waves lapped the shore in a blatant mating ritual
winking in communion, birds joyously expressed their
anticipation over the changing seasons, and other
creatures carried on daily conversations I observed
with awestruck wonder. Nature played an exquisite
symphony with each musician an instrument in the
perfectly harmonizing masterpiece—the wind rustling
through the trees, a babbling brook, the call of the gulls,
a thunderstorm, waves crashing to shore, a crackling
fire, the hooting of an owl, and the loud call of cicadas.
I continually wrote about these tunes with endless
fervor since they were my soul's music, suffusing me in
such elation I rose out of my body as our frequencies
seamlessly united to flow as one melody. When I was
entirely lost in nature I literally became the pounding
surf, gentle breeze or sparrow proclaiming its tune
from the branch of a tree—simply merging into the
entirety of the larger life source as we synthesized.
It was an out-of-body experience I craved more
than breath itself, as I transcended the unrelenting
bleakness of my own mortality to a realm where
promise reigned supreme. And then I was inevitably
commanded back down to reality where I was painfully

distinct and never felt I belonged or was bound to any one or thing. I was then simply suffused in my own horrible sense of desperation and entirely alone.

I understood the call of nature as well as the cry of my own heart, as it was deep in my soul and a stalwart ally throughout life's journey. As such, we had true empathy for each other's needs. I appreciated nature's challenges and was careful to honor its mystery as no human ever could, and nature respected me in a way no person ever could—understanding how desperately I craved solace and kinship and opening its arms to offer much needed comfort. There was such magic in nature's intricate web, and I was in utter astonishment of the gifts it manifested every single day.

Other than general despair, I contemplated nature's haunting melody and ethereal beauty more than any other theme, truly awed by its wonders which never ceased to amaze me. I was most alive and in my flow when immersed in nature, completely outside my burdensome head with senses engaged and standing in rapt attention. My entire being craved the peace, quiescence and elaborate simplicity of the outside world, first documenting the spell it cast at a very young age with no more impactful influence throughout life. I depended on nature to rescue my heavy head from endless worrying, ruminating and overthinking, ushering in calm and moving me into my heart to find peace. It was the only environment

*I understood
the call of nature
as well as the cry
of my own heart,
as it was deep
in my soul and
a stalwart ally
throughout
life's journey.*

capable of offering consolation from the moment I entered its spellbinding portal.

I was continually moved to tears by seeing examples of nature's beauty everywhere—water sparkling with sunlight's reflection, colors of a sunrise or sunset, hues of fall leaves, glow of a fire's embers, the intricate pistil of a flower, the design of a spider web, and the vastness of a starlit sky, to name a few. Becoming transfixed with these miracles and utterly enmeshed in their vibrant colors and patterns made me long to merge into their expansiveness.

Collecting bits of nature's bounty and holding them like precious jewels connected me to the grandeur of our cosmos in bringing concreteness to the ephemerality of life. The beauty of a leaf dressed in its fall finery before traveling to its demise was enough to make my heart ache. The brilliant colors of a sunrise tellin shell ushered in reverence with such organic creation birthed before my very eyes. I marveled at Earth's treasures, using the words *awe, wonder* and *amazement* in describing their exquisite beauty. The potential of discovery in nature, knowing it was ever-changing in a state of perpetual rebirth, carried tremendous promise. For one never knew what magnificent jewel might reveal itself if we kept our eyes open, staying curious and aware. *How analogous was this to life in general if we truly adopted this mindset?*

Given I stood in reverence of nature's innumerable gifts, it was shocking that others were utterly blind to the extraordinary wonder right before their eyes. How could they walk the same path and not see the same beauty—rushing swiftly by the miracle of life? How could they never truly open their eyes and stop to "*smell the flowers*," appreciating the simple, yet most profound joys along the way? This was tragic, for as Marcel Proust recognized: "*The real voyage of discovery consists not in seeking new landscapes, but in having new eyes.*" And yet, here I was judging others while just as guilty in hurtling through life without pause, still so time and achievement focused I feared becoming intoxicated with the view and losing sight of accomplishing clear objectives.

I was continually struck by the vastness of nature's interconnected system and the seamless manner in which it functioned, juxtaposed against my discrete insignificance. Being simply an observer in the center of this boundless ecosystem, aware of just how much was occurring without my involvement, put my overblown sense of importance into perspective. In the realm of this perfectly tuned machine existing well before and well after me, my problems were minuscule and my presence unnecessary. It certainly embraced me as an observer, but was perfectly capable of playing its poignant song alone. While in one sense devastating, I simultaneously felt my smallness to be reassuring as it lifted the burden of responsibility off my shoulders, allowing me to revel in being a spectator with no skin in the game. No matter my behavior or actions, the seasons would continue changing and time would march on. I could rejoice in that continuity absent all personal performance anxiety. Nature had already achieved perfection without my assistance and would continue to do so evermore.

There were multitudes of metaphors in nature relating to my earthly experience. At times when I beheld a beautiful shell and stooped to pick it up, a wave would furtively dance under my fingertips and swiftly carry it out to sea. And I would remain dumbfounded, certain I had lost the most precious gift ever. Yet I gradually came to see that what nature gives us can just as easily be taken away, and we ultimately needed to accept that as part of life without lamentation. Likewise, just as nature opened its arms to offer solace, it also demonstrated sheer wrath and could devastate with one blow. It was quite synonymous with our power as people to positively impact others and perform great good, but also wreak havoc with our latent contempt. And although humans ever attempted to exert their muscle and tame nature's might, it longed for freedom from oppression and to rage as openly and unencumbered as I.

Of all seasons, autumn was the most sacred time of year for me. Something about leaves changing colors and "*drying up*" as if aging, then traveling to Earth in

their death march illustrated a powerful life metaphor. I had always believed trees were grieving as their leaves fell to the ground each autumn, having been rendered naked in such a public and humiliating manner. But I also understood this process from the perspective of the leaves themselves, who were actually "*leaving*" their lifetime homes and falling to their demise. I imagined that's why they were called leaves in the first place—because they ultimately left their mother tree to experience dissolution and eventual rebirth. I found it fascinating these leaves had spent their days so vibrant and alive on limb, yet the moment they separated from their life source were approaching mortality. And once touching ground, immediately began a new process in both their decay in leaving one life form, and rebirth in decomposition into the earth to become another. Witnessing such a vivid depiction of the life cycle playing out so boldly in front of me made me insistent on becoming enmeshed in it. And after ruminating on this process throughout my entire childhood, I decided to inject myself right into the middle of it in adulthood.

One crisp autumn day I escaped to my front yard full of maple trees, attempting to catch their leaves as they fell from branches before they hit earth. That very trip from branch to ground represented the gray space between life and death—the tunnel of light, so to speak. And I believed if I could catch even one single leaf in the midst of its final journey to wish it well and

*There was such
profound hope
and promise in
nature—and
perpetual rebirth.*

give it a proper send-off, I would become part of the life and death process itself. It was a deeply spiritual exercise and made me feel incredibly alive. There was such profound hope and promise in nature—and perpetual rebirth. The leaves were ending their life as a tree, yet would soon rise up as something living but in entirely different form. That filled me with tremendous optimism, as I longed to experience this same metamorphosis once I transcended my human body.

It was actually quite difficult catching leaves as they twisted and turned their way to the ground—especially when windy, as autumn days tended to be. However, if I was fortunate enough to do so, I would tenderly hold the leaf in both hands, giving it a gentle kiss before placing it to rest on the ground. For my children who ultimately joined me in this mystical ritual, we added the additional step of making a wish while holding the leaf in solemn homage before lowering it to rest. I found this act profoundly meaningful and further deepening my connection to nature, truly compelled to understand this mysterious life cycle.

As with nature, I had a similar connection to both instrumental and "*bodily*" music as well. I knew every one of us to be a living symphony with multitudes of organic sounds and tempos emanating from our bodies, each proclaiming its own unique tone and beat. I relished examining others as they went about their daily lives to sense their rhythms, some so fluid and

effortless—in musical terms they were "*andante*"—and
others quite choppy, forced and rushed—more of a
"*mosso*." Some were "*largo*"—quite slow and method-
ical—and others in a seemingly all-out race—a "*presto*"
or "*prestissimo*"—to arrive at their finale. I always
envisioned gathering a group of individuals together
and amplifying their internal symphonies, eager to hear
if their singular melodies would orchestrate and what
extraordinary tune might resound. How fascinating
life itself was simultaneously beating externally through
nature and internally through our bodies, playing truly
organic concertos that would ultimately merge into the
universe once our tangible forms expired.

The over-excitability of my senses was a continual
challenge to navigate, making it difficult to appear
"*normal*" and find my place in the world. But as long as I
could effectively hide these eccentricities and operate in
a relatively inconspicuous manner, my hypersensitivity
also made everyday engagements truly miraculous. I
reveled in experiencing life so deeply and derived
such pleasure from nature, music, literature, poetry,
food and art. I could be promptly moved to tears in
hearing strains of a poignant song, tasting the first
vine-ripened tomatoes of summer, beholding a sunrise
over the mountaintops, witnessing stars grace the sky,
smelling a rose with dewdrops on its petals, or viewing
a ladybug with crushed wing struggling to fly—wholly

engrossed in the experience, extracting every ounce
of feeling imaginable. I was the thunder, I was
the budding flower, and I was the fish swimming
gracefully in the pond. The euphoria over *"becoming
one"* with the universe was utterly excruciating, as I
felt communion with all beings envelop me in a deep
sense of belonging. For when I harmonized with
music, nature or any other truly palpable experience,
the clamor in my head subsided and I was free to
soar. And although I didn't enjoy physical contact, I
loved rubbing the rough bark of a tree, letting sand
sift through my fingers, or caressing stunning objects
d'art, feeling my heart race when touching them.
Being invigorated by absolute sensory engagement
instantly lifted me above my churning head and
repressed body, with my soul wholly transcending the
painful reality of earthly life to join in concert with
the cosmos.

If you take the time to listen
To waves crashing on the shore
Breezes rustling through the leaves
Or birds calling as they soar
You will surely realize nature
Speaks a language all its own
Ever tempting us to enter
Its vast depths with tales unknown

The salt air, surf and sea breeze
Grant elixir to the soul
As I wander this idyllic stretch
With no intent or goal
For the intrigue of the ocean
With its treasures to explore
Leave me yearning to remain here
Ever hungering for more

Spring's first shoots are poised for action
In response to nature's cue
Keen to rouse themselves from slumber
And exultantly break through
Having battled through the winter
Trapped beneath the frozen earth
Armed to greet the world triumphant
In this miracle of birth

———

The more I walk
These well-worn paths
The more I truly see
Finding every day
A novel view
Unfurls in front of me

This ever-changing landscape
Brings an unexpected view
Every time I gaze upon it
Manifesting sights anew

———

The vision of fall's masterpiece
Has faded into earth
Though I hope to see it rise again
As part of spring's rebirth

So much of nature speaks
In songs and sounds instead of words
Yet expresses just as poignantly—
Just listen to the birds!

——

How I long to be a songbird
Serenading from the tree
Boldly chirping my same warble
Every day repeatedly
Unperturbed with how the world
Perceives that pithy little tune
Flush with freedom to proclaim
My unaffected, humble croon

A bird was chirping gleefully
Outside my window pane
Although I could only hear its song
And grimace with disdain
For what yesterday resounded
As a joyful melody
Was now heard through desolation
As a bleak cacophony

———

Oh how I wish
I'd see today
A sign that spring
Is on its way
It seems like ages
Since I've heard
The twitter
Of a mockingbird

Affront this bright
And crackling fire
I'm spellbound watching
Flames stretch higher
Till the winter's
Coldest days
Are kindled by
Spring's brilliant rays

My heart aches for this feeble fire
Longing to stretch limbs much higher
Jailed behind glass doors for show
With just one log to fuel its glow
Existing as a passive flame
Condemned to bear a life so tame

The sun just beginning to filter
Through the leaves straining toward its warm light
As I wrestle my pillow in combat
Fallen prey of a long, sleepless night
Swiftly tiptoeing out the bedroom
Brow furrowed in utter frustration
I slip soundlessly from confinement
In search of sustained contemplation
The waves pound the rocks with great fervor
As I near the secluded place
Awash in anticipation
Free to wholly absorb this vast space
Soon I'm basking in the stillness
As it soothes this rigid frame
Unweaving the threads of vexation
Not caring my status or name
Infusing these lungs with such vigor
Neither head nor limbs ache any longer
The arduous burden of duty
Replaced by a feeling much stronger
Alive with a heightened perception

continues »

Of a world I've no power to shape
With such gratitude for Mother Nature
Who delivered this private escape
Moved no longer by obligations
From which I'm unable to leave
For suddenly cast an observer
With no role or intent to achieve
Consumed not with yesterday's losses
Or tomorrow's innumerable trials
Guided now by the rashness of breakers
And pure solace which stretches for miles

Though I'm thoroughly enraptured
By these vibrant autumn days
Once dead leaves adorn the ground
I grow afflicted with malaise
Having drawn great inspiration
From such captivating hues
But now brace myself for winter
Prompting agonizing blues

———

Just days ago I raised my face
To welcome summer's warm embrace
Today I linger to prolong
The strains of fall's once vivid song
Tomorrow wool will swathe my form
And through the winter keep it warm
To revel in rebirth of spring
Extolling change the seasons bring

The tree outside my window grieves
As teardrops masquerade as leaves
Cascading till they soak the ground
And though my friend makes not a sound
Its branches bow in deep despair
Forsaken through the winter bare

———

How fast
The autumn leaves do fall
Yet render not a sound
Till the trees
Are wearing none at all
And let them dress the ground

———

The trees once cloaked in brilliant hues
Now bow their limbs in grief
As the wind exhales its bid farewell
In ode to simple leaf

It takes focus, faith and patience
To find treasures on the sand
When so many have been ravaged
By the ocean's mighty hand
And requires scanning thousands
To unearth a precious few
But that separates explorers
From the others racing through

———

The waves so gently
Lap the shore
Then hasten back
To ask for more
And I can only
Sit and stare
Witness to such
A strange affair

Just this morning I observed a shell
Within a tidal pool
Promptly hastening to kidnap
This rare, iridescent jewel
As I reveled in good fortune
Having never found before
Such a prize for my collection
On this quiet stretch of shore
But no sooner did I place it
On my bureau for display
Did I notice it was moving
And acknowledge with dismay
This extraordinary gift
Was never mine to truly own
But bequeathed to its inhabitant
To guard its fate alone

The morning sun
Softly frames my face
A breeze lightly blows
And my worries erase
As the fragrant sea air
Gently tickles my nose
With the warmth of the sand
Like silk gloves on my toes
The bold call of the gulls
As they swoop through the sky
Has me yearning to soar
Without needing to try
Every crash of the waves
And each pull of the tide
Offer freedom at last
To cast all cares aside
For the rush of each day
Just a blur in my mind
With peace now my only
Intention to find

Today I watched a gull
Attempt to break an oyster shell
As it dropped onto the pavement
For its contents to expel
Yet when utterly intact
She picked it up and tried again
For a total of three times
Until the prize was discharged then
Now I wonder why we humans
Must succeed on every try
While our feathered friends keep striving
Even when life goes awry

Grass chides the haughty leaves
Who flaunt their verve from limb on high
Warning: "I'll be meeting all of you
For fall is closely nigh"

—

Leaves reproach the grassy floor
Content to gloat from limb on high
"We will never come together
Till the end is truly nigh"

When a leaf encounters ground
It has exhaled its final breath
Having plummeted from limb on high
To no uncertain death

———

One day content on outstretched limbs
Which scrape the clear blue skies
And the next inhaling final breaths
En route to their demise

Though judging by the time of year
The winter should indeed be here
Such balmy air and clear blue skies
Would lead one to think otherwise
And given the delighted smiles
Of those enjoying nature's wiles
It's safe to say few would resist
Rejoicing should this warmth persist

—

I would rather be a rock
Than fragrant flower flush in bloom
For a rock remains unchanged
Long after blossoms face their doom

I venture down this winding road
Now freed from my austere abode
Amidst the trees and tangled brush
Forgotten is the city rush
And for this brief unbroken time
Delighting in a world sublime
I hope that visions of this place
Extend throughout the week I face

On this brisk
November morning
I escape
Without a warning
Down to meet
The untamed sea
For at peace
I long to be
Agitated on my perch
Watching breakers
Roar and lurch
Seagulls swooping
High and low
And crabs scuttling
To and fro
All completely
Unaware
That I'm drowning
In despair
For I seek

continues »

Accord in vain
From what's blank
Of heart and brain
Thereby leaving
Waves at play
To expunge
My steps today

We perform a vital concert
An organic, streaming song
That invites our body instruments
To join and play along
From inflections of our crying
To pulsating of the heart
With the rhythm of our breathing
Spaced so evenly apart
The quick tempo of eye blinking
And the cadence of our gait
The rich timbre of deep sighing
Tones of words we formulate
The firm pattern of our chewing
And the pitch of ringing ears
The loud chorus of our stomachs
And the tracks made by our tears
Forge a masterful arrangement
Synthesizing through our days
Fate conducting every movement
And duration life's tune plays

When I strummed my first guitar
I was enthralled by its vibration
Vaulted to a realm afar
Where sound and soul joined in elation
With intoxicating feeling
Born from synchronicity
Swiftly morphing angst to healing
Through euphoric harmony

———

Though I spent my days beach combing
For that one elusive shell
To complete my rare collection
On the hallowed shelf to dwell
I was never truly searching
For an undisputed prize
Rather using Mother Nature
To assuage my heartfelt cries
Since the riches I desired
Were still buried in my soul
Needing vigilant exhuming
To reach concord with the whole

Simply opening our eyes
To nature's vibrant mystery
Gives us reason to stop doing
And embrace what's here to see

———

I silently escape from bed
And brush the cobwebs from my head
Then out the door without a peep
While unaware all others sleep
To circle round our block until
I've warded off the winter chill
Transfixed as shades of pink and blue
Proclaim the morning's grand debut
And glimmers of sun's dazzling rays
Are welcomed with my humble praise

If we harmonize with nature
As it plays its poignant song
We'll soar far beyond ourselves
And to the universe belong

———

When I wake to sounds of thunder
And the beating of the rain
Endless rivulets of water
Streaming down my windowpane
I am thankful for the shelter
That protects my fragile form
And assuages me right back to sleep
Despite the raging storm

There's no anarchy in nature
Just within the human mind
For the cosmos never seeks
To act malicious or unkind
And accepts the way it is
Without intention or control
Quite content to simply "be"
Despite no predetermined goal

———

When I'm taken by a tune
I swiftly slip into a trance
So enraptured by the music
I'm compelled to sing and dance
With no fear of denigration
Or compulsion to conform
Guided solely by the rhythm
And disdain for social norm

There is nothing more enticing
Than the shoreline at low tide
Proudly brandishing its treasures
With no secrets left to hide
As I scramble to and fro
Resolved to wipe the canvas clean
So the waves don't do it for me
Bound to forge a fresh, new scene

———

Hearing is quite passive
For we grow immune to sound
Spending much of life oblivious
To anthems all around
Whereas listening is conscious
And requires full attention
To connect us with the world
Where every song rings in ascension

Every time the waves
Caress the shore and pull away
They deposit newfound treasures
And sweep other ones away

———

I can comb this vibrant shoreline
Up and down for hours each day
For the waves keep leaving presents
To augment my vast array

———

We must scurry to pluck riches
Off the jewel-laden sand
Since the waves will soon rage through
And take them back as nature planned

I long to be as constant
As the waves that crash to shore
Never losing my momentum
Through what nature has in store

———

I long to be as giddy
As this ever flowing stream
Dancing freely down the mountainside
With no intent or scheme

———

How I yearn to be the river
Flowing down the mountainside
Simply focused on my journey
And delighting in the ride

The lazy days of sun and surf
Of sand and gentle breeze
Cause these summer months to hasten
Leaving countless memories

———

I wonder if these treasures
Boldly plucked right off the sand
Would prefer remaining pummeled
By the ocean's mighty hand
Or abducted to a new home
Far beyond the breakers roar
To lie dormant on a shelf
Immune to climate evermore

I'm transported
By the waves
That ebb and flow within the ocean
Though waves also
Flood my soul
When bearing sound or deep emotion

———

Oh water I must ask you
Why you ever rush away
I'm unsure where you'd be racing to
On such a lovely day
Though I understand that rivers
Must have obligations too
Life should never be this stressful
So relax, enjoy the view
At the frantic pace you're running
You'll be early I dare say
And neglect this fleeting chance
To see the sights along the way

Hiking verdant mountain trails
Or simply gazing at the sea
Lift me far above dejection
Where both head and heart are free

———

I can count eleven layers
Though there surely may be more
For there never is an end
To mountain stretches to explore

———

It gently fell
Throughout the night
When much to my surprise
Fresh snow glinting
In the morning light
Aroused my sleep-filled eyes

———

As I sip crisp mountain air
Amid the rustling aspen trees
My heart soars just like the wrens
Uplifted on the bracing breeze

I'm enraptured by the views
Which stretch beyond where I can see
And absolve my heart to soar
Up where it truly longs to be

——

These views are as expansive
As the reaches of my mind
Which is why I visit often
Knowing solace I will find

I am baffled why the crow
Proclaims the same tune every day
Absent fear of disrespect
With nothing more profound to say

———

The cheerful chirping
Of a bird
A joyous sound
The first time heard
But when its song
Becomes well-known
The days assume
A wistful tone
As soon its tune
Will cease to ring
Until we circle
Back to spring

A woodpecker is pecking
On the post outside my door
But I've not the nerve to tell him
It's not his tree anymore

His absorption is quite striking
Simply whittling from the heart
I'm in awe of this great master
Nimbly crafting novel art

Yet he doesn't note my presence
And I give no cause for fear
Blind to frivolous distraction
With intent to persevere

Could I ever grow resentful
Of a creature bold and skilled
When I'm ever wishing humans
Were as steadfast and strong-willed?

How can nature be resigned
To what is destined every year
And look passing in the eye
Without uncertainty or fear?

—

If you gaze inside a tree
You'll witness more than just its bark
For creation's mastermind
Has absolutely hit the mark
With this brilliant tour du force
Whose grandeur no one can deny
As such miracles of nature
Offer more than meet the eye

A tree remains a tree
And never seeks to be a rose
Since the cosmos just accepts what is
With no intent to pose

———

Nature doesn't try to change
Whatever is to be
In allowing blooms to wither
Not find immortality

———

Nature doesn't modify
Whatever it cannot
For a tree will still parade its bark
Once it begins to rot

A dahlia doesn't care to be
More stunning than the rose
Rather honors Mother Nature
And whatever she bestows

———

A gentle breeze
Revives the trees
As still as was the air
And arouses those
Whose pleasure shows
With smiles and tousled hair

Sunlight sifting through the leaves
Casts stained glass windows on the ground
While the world moves swiftly by
And I gape utterly spellbound

—

Nature brandishes such splendor
For our eyes to plainly see
If we take the time to revel
In her simple majesty

There's a magic that suffuses me
The moment I arrive
As my tensions melt away
And I feel utterly alive
For the pounding of the breakers
And the cleansing salt-air breeze
Lift me far above all discord
With their power to appease

—

Some days this sandy stretch
Is an enticing candy store
Overflowing with abundance
And delights to grab galore
Yet on others this same coastline
Leaves us little to collect
But the simple admonition
To receive and not expect

I found the most exquisite shell
Upon the sand today
Yet when I knelt down to pick it up
A wave got in the way
Swiftly bringing it right out to sea
While I remained aghast
For what Mother Nature gives us
She can take back just as fast

POWERLESSNESS

Existential angst brought a profound loss of control
over mortality and continual sense I was being pulled
by an overwhelming force, rendering me unable
to regulate daily life. Although attempting to resist its
might, I was powerless as it had me by the throat dragging
me against my will. I was isolated from humanity,
painfully focused on my smallness in the vast space of
existence and wallowing in futility. Despite my desperate
efforts, I would never impact fate and attain immortality,
ultimately snuffed out by an uninvited death. Life was
in vain and my brief time spent here on Earth would
go unnoticed.

This force manifested itself as a terrifying demon insistent
on punishing me and disallowing pleasure, looming day
and night and deriding my every attempt to exist simply
as I was. The demon was never satisfied with just *"being,"*
rather entirely focused on imperfection and magnifying
flaws, overlooking strengths and operating under a
distorted all-or-nothing mentality. It made me feel
worthless in the deepest sense with constant awareness
I wasn't good enough and would never be good enough,
and must fight to change who I was. This monster
rendered me utterly defenseless in directing all moves
and showing no mercy toward the weak, vulnerable
soul pleading for freedom. It continually demanded I
must *"be the best"* through attaining perfection in all
pursuits: popular by being socially accepted, thinner
by eating less, wealthier by spending less, healthier by
exercising more, smarter by studying more and successful

by achieving more and performing better. It also demanded I participate in every activity possible for fear I would miss out on a momentous experience. It was a chain around my neck being pulled tighter with each passing day.

I was entirely incapable of stopping this internal tyrant—petrified if I thought life was too good, felt joy or showed myself to be openly happy it would strike me down. I therefore took great care to never openly engage in frivolity, fearing tragedy would ensue. And although I was truly grateful for the blessings in my life, the demon wouldn't let me remain content with being thankful, continually warning doom was lurking and I must *"make something of myself before it was too late."* I therefore felt the urgent need to keep performing, all the while appearing miserable so as not to attract disaster, since it seemed misfortune always befell those who were happiest. After all, headlines always depicted, "___ *had everything. And then, (drum roll) tragedy struck..."*

This insidious inner force was relentless and had me in its shackles, demanding I perform prescribed orders, accomplish missions, and overcome challenges or I would perish. I therefore became paranoid, obsessed and superstitious at a very young age; pursuing innumerable commanded directives if correctly executed would shield me from the demon and death, and if not, portend a catastrophic end. For starters, the demon

I was entirely
incapable of stopping
this internal tyrant—
petrified if I thought
life was too good,
felt joy or showed
myself to be openly
happy it would strike
me down.

continually mandated a certain placement of items to govern my fate. I'd be lying in my bed, see the closet door partly open and messaged, *"unless I close the door something bad will happen."* I'd then drag myself out of bed and close the closet door. But no sooner did I get back into bed I'd see something else—the way a doll was positioned or picture was hanging, compelling me to get up again and again to adjust them. I despised needing to *"right"* objects in my environment, because once I started *"fixing,"* the ritual could continue for hours. Likewise, I would be advised if I wore certain articles of clothing my peers would or wouldn't befriend me, or I would stay healthy or become sick. These generally weren't even garments others could see; for instance, I believed if I wore a certain pair of socks the boy I liked would like me back—and if I didn't, he wouldn't. I was also compelled to play mind games while walking, certain if I didn't reach a specified building by the time I counted to ten one of my relatives would die or I would become paralyzed in a horrific car accident. I also followed the same pattern with school related pressures like elections or exams—if we didn't pass three white cars by the time I arrived at school I would lose the election or fail the test. It was never-ending and thoroughly exhausting.

Other challenges were more difficult to overcome. For instance, if I could hold my breath for three minutes straight I would live to see my next

birthday, or if I didn't blink for 60 seconds I would
be granted one wish that would come true. If I made
three basketball shots in a row I'd become friends with
someone popular and if not, remain a social outcast. Or
if I steered my bicycle correctly to ride over a particular
small pebble ahead on the pathway, or hit a certain tree
with a rock, I would have a blissful marriage; if not,
suffer an acrimonious divorce. Another peculiarity
was if I could guess the exact outside temperature
first thing in the morning I would have a trouble-free
day. Likewise, seeing a digital clock change from :59
to :00 was also an excellent omen—ideally witnessing
9:59 turn to 10:00 (since that involved three numbers
morphing into four) without blinking meant I would
remain healthy for the subsequent 21 days. And lastly,
finding a coin on the street was an incredible boon
and brought about great relief knowing I would be
protected against adversity for days to come. However,
it could only be acquired heads up, then placed
immediately into my sock with the head side touching
my skin, in order for good fortune to manifest. I was
riddled with rituals and superstitions designed to allay
this overwhelming sense of powerlessness and keep me
safe from ever-imminent threats.

Although potentially bringing a certain sense of
order over the uncontrollable elements of life, these
compulsions were incredibly burdensome, ultimately
pushing me even further inside my frenzied head which

impeded living fully and freely. Yet they emerged
over helplessness to control the future and forestall
tragedy, comrades in forging order from chaos and
protection from the demon threatening denunciation.
In fact, even today with decades past I still find myself
believing random, innocuous signs will determine
outcomes over which I have little control but am
desperate to achieve.

I was absolutely terrorized by the intensity of that inner
demon threatening condemnation for weakness.
I could never reconcile the two living, breathing beings
coexisting inside—the sweet, innocent child who simply
wished to be kind, honest, and live happily on her own
terms, and the evil, ruthless tyrant determined to take
advantage of that gentle, considerate being by forcing it
to suffer. That tyrant drove me to the brink of collapse
every single day, demanding I keep moving when
I simply needed to rest, starve myself when I desperately wanted to eat, rabidly study when I yearned to
have fun, and hoard money when I wished to indulge
myself. The demon set up lofty goals for the good
person to accomplish, prohibiting her from stopping
until she succeeded despite their magnitude (such as
you must get straight A's on every single assignment
and test throughout college). And if she fell even
slightly short of perfection, the monster would castigate
her. Yet my timid self never had the courage to stand
up and retort, *"I don't have to follow your orders and don't
care what you think!"* My submissive self was simply too

terrified of challenging the seething tyrant, therefore compelled to continue behaving exactly as requested so as not to further enrage it.

Living with this omnipresent terror felt as if a tidal wave was ever looming, although I desperately wanted to escape the impending breakers. And yet the surge was growing larger and more forceful, intent on submerging me despite using every bit of available strength to remain afloat. The pain of feeling and caring too much was suffocating my soul. I wished I wasn't so consumed with dying, I wished I didn't care so much about others' opinions, I wished I didn't take everything so personally, and I wished I could just let go of my fears and stop perseverating. I also wished my relationships were better, but simply couldn't alter these circumstances or escape their grip. When I started losing control, all my worst fears surfaced, and no matter where I tried to hide they were menacing. Suddenly I was terrified of everything outside my control—dying in a crash, being murdered, getting cancer, losing my faculties, achieving nothing of significance; everything I couldn't control began consuming me. Then my head would start spinning and I'd work myself into such hysteria I couldn't eat, sleep or even drag myself out of bed each morning. Ultimately, this rabid need for order moved me to exert control over as many life aspects as possible to feel safe, but I ended up deploying some extremely unhealthy, dangerous, all-or-nothing, and merciless behaviors.

Sometimes I felt so overwhelmed I didn't even want to change my clothes or shower, closing myself up entirely to escape from the world.

Sometimes I felt so overwhelmed I didn't even want to change my clothes or shower, closing myself up entirely to escape from the world. Although I smelled terrible and my hair was greasy, I still refrained from getting into the shower, feeling safer in the same dirty clothes as long as they kept me unexposed. Since there was no resolution to my fears—after all no one could ever ensure me I wasn't going to be the victim of a terrible accident or contract an incurable disease—the anxiety never subsided. Sure, I could continue on with life like everyone else, remaining totally oblivious to impending threats, but these potential catastrophes were ever-present and the possibility of them occurring never abated. But the worst part of all was the guilt I endured for letting life elapse without truly enjoying each moment, disgusted with my inability to take control and break free. I often wrote about the duplicity of wanting to live and wanting to die, and truly aching to feel hopeful yet reality inevitably getting the best of me.

As a young girl at age eight I wrote the following journal entry: *"Do we ever get to the point of feeling satisfied and at peace with ourselves and our lives? Is there ever a time we stop questioning, seeking, regretting, doubting, reflecting, second-guessing and hoping? And if so, do we know when we've arrived? Or do we continually keep searching only to end up more confused than when we started? Should we perhaps give up even before we begin and never enter the race at all? Or are we just too stupid* to realize the struggle is futile? How I wish someone could simply whisper in my ear, 'please, rest easy, because it's worth the fight.' For if it's not worth the fight I could die tomorrow without having truly lived. I guess I'll never know, meaning I'm doomed to continue trudging on, not knowing where it will lead or if I'll ever find solace."

Another journal entry from age 12 lamented: "What is it in me that won't let me rest, enjoy, and remain content with just being still? Why do I continually question, ponder and churn thoughts over and over in my mind until I become so confused I have no idea what I've even been thinking? I am not a theologian or philosopher. I have no desire to be constantly engaged in rumination— brow furrowed, shoulders stooped and muttering as I plod along. I am just an ordinary girl desperate to lead a carefree, laughter-filled life. Why can't I just speak without second-guessing my comments for days on end and express my feelings as I feel them? Why can't I just enjoy the current moment without worrying about what tragedy may hit me tomorrow? How does one stop feeling so much? I am drowning in a sea of emotions and cannot bear it any longer!"

Continual analysis also led me to develop very vivid mental pictures and expectations of "how situations were supposed to unfold," which ultimately set me up for profound disappointment. I so compellingly believed "what was right," that I was inevitably betrayed and disillusioned. This made coming to terms with realities so far from my assumptions and reconciling them with my strong imprint of *"what should be"* an ongoing challenge. And in my household, events never played out according to expectation, leaving me entirely unfulfilled. How it *should* be seemed so obvious, but life never delivered what I envisioned and I had no one with whom to share this sense of disillusionment. And tragically, such early and intense disappointment with the actions and behaviors of those closest to me morphed into deep cynicism toward all humanity, forging an entrenched belief system based on these unwavering perceptions of the world. In sum, my irrational precepts became the following:

» I will always be alone and can trust no one.

» People are selfish and will blindly hurt me in order to elevate themselves.

» I am unworthy of love, kindness, gratification and pleasure.

» Life is meant to be a fairy tale of uninterrupted bliss.

» I must perform perfectly. Achieving less than 100% is unacceptable.

» When circumstances don't go as expected, outcomes are never rectifiable.

» Happiness is caused by other events and people, not in my control or dependent on how I act or think.

» Failures are shaming, requiring self-punishment and contempt. Nothing good ever comes from failure.

» People aren't valued for who they are, just for what they accomplish.

» Events occurring in the past determine the future.

» I am worthless unless I mirror in looks and behavior my image of perfection and am accepted by the highest status individuals.

» No one is *"on my side,"* rather adversaries to compete against and defeat.

» The future is to be feared and the past lamented.

» There is no meaning or purpose to life and our actions will ultimately be for naught.

These horrible misperceptions led me to catastrophize situations and engage in scathing criticism of both myself and others for our collective inability to reach unrealistic expectations. I find it sobering to read these statements today, for their extremity fostered my acute negativity and ensuing depression. But during the first few decades of life, these beliefs were my reality and I didn't see them as unreasonable or inappropriate whatsoever. In fact, becoming so dogmatic in this thinking prevented anyone or anything from convincing me otherwise, ignoring examples or acts disproving my theories. This belief system inevitably left me resentful and floundering in misery, thinking either: *"I'm never going to feel happiness and forever remain a social outcast,"* OR *"life isn't fair,"* perpetually railing against my fate and circumstances beyond my control. And utter helplessness eventually evolved into unrelenting despair.

The derivation of this mania also involved a large measure of self-loathing. I despised myself for failing to win the love of my parents and exemplify both inside and outside characteristics I was desperate to manifest to the world: extreme beauty, ease in relationships, brilliance to excel in all disciplines, and confidence to be comfortably me. And since there was nothing I could do to become someone else, I wanted to destroy the person I was for my inability to do so. Inflicting such abuse became quite simple in denying my body any material sustenance or pleasure, as it rapidly removed all hope from daily living and created maniacal focus on pure survival. And that obsessive fixation on the basic and trivial inputs into and outputs from my body essentially took the pressure off worrying about greater issues entirely beyond my control.

In reality, I had become so consumed with thwarting mortality that I was unable to truly live, existing in a trance-like stupor and powerless to control my thoughts and feelings. And although aware enough to know I didn't want to continue in this manner, I was helpless to ease the pain and perpetually questioned the meaning of existence. In fact, the thought of spending even one more day feeling such despondency was enough to impel drastic action, and I continually envisioned renouncing the battle through taking my life. It had become increasingly clear why individuals resorted to vices like alcohol, drugs and suicide to dull/ end the pain, since my own feelings of hopelessness were so overwhelming I was apt to do just about anything to relieve them.

I was ultimately left with the contention I was entirely alone, drowning in anguish with little strength or reason to emerge from seclusion. I just couldn't seem to control emotions so rapidly descending to the lowest levels imaginable, and this inability to improve either my state or fate left me terribly unsettled with a devastating sense of futility. And yet, I knew there *must* be reason for the despair plaguing me and was desperate to disclose its purpose. Only then would I find courage to keep on. For if I didn't receive that answer, I'd be doomed to perpetual darkness and eventually surrender, knowing I couldn't live shackled by misery much longer...

What happened to that inner child
Who used to run so free
Quite content to while away the hours
Exploring joyfully
Who embraced life with abandon
Quick to laugh, dance, skip and sing
Always eager for adventure
Never fearing any thing
What happened to that inner child
Who dreamed without a care
Bound by pure imagination
Finding promise everywhere
Who accepted any challenge
Never focused on the goal
With the fortitude to try again
Unfettered by control
What happened to that inner child
Who simply loved to play

continues »

Roaming bravely through the neighborhood
With nothing in her way
What happened to that inner child
So confident and bright
Is she aged and stopped believing
In the power of her might

Guilt is wasted spirit
That confines us in the past
In a chapter long completed
With the characters all cast
And serves no compelling purpose
Since we can't change history
So let's focus on the present
And allow bygones to be

———

I am crippled by ambivalence
Afflicted with despair
Agonized by desperation
And discomfited with care
Overwhelmed by hesitation
Ever longing for relief
From the guilt that my decisions
May have caused another grief

While the rest are seeking pleasure
I am reveling in pain
For I'm loathe to spend a lifetime
Chasing ecstasy in vain

———

My heart simply wants to play
But my head gets in the way
In demanding I abstain
Since indulgence is in vain

———

My mind longs to dance
And my heart yearns to sing
Yet I've locked them in a cage
Afraid to covet anything

———

I welcome despair
But all pleasure resist
Crouched alone in the dark
Where it's safe to exist

Our innately human tendency
Is needing to control
Molding actions and our beings
Into rigid plans or role
And unless that grip on order
Is permitted to release
We will never know ourselves
Or access everlasting peace

———

I suppressed unbridled terror
Locking fiends in caverns deep
Single-mindedly protecting
My dark secrets bound to keep
Quite convinced with full detention
They would never rise again
And my life would flow serenely
Truly liberated then
But believing beasts were gone for good
Was not so smart indeed
Since by then their roots had taken hold
Advancing like a weed

We can lodge blame at our parents
For their disrespectful ways
But that's nothing close to how
We cruelly treat ourselves most days

———

My mind is never willing
To just settle down and be
For it feels the constant urge
To judge, berate and torment me

———

As long as we delude ourselves
With how we wish to be
We will never know salvation
Since surrender sets us free

What should we be expecting
When our lives end and we die
Will we reunite with loved ones
From a castle in the sky?
Will we feel a sense of solace
That extends outside all form
Basking in transcendent light
Forever comforted and warm?
Or instead will all we know
Just simply vanish in one breath
With no sense of hope beyond
The utter certitude of death?

———

In death do we return
To floating gently in the womb?
Or does darkness overwhelm
And leave us rotting in a tomb?
Or do angels lead the way
Into a luminescent light?
I'll be searching for that answer
Till I say my last good night

I met despair
Down where she lives
And stared her in the eye
Left abandoned
In my nakedness
No strength left to deny
Bid adieu to comrades
Want and hope
To walk this path alone
For it's here I'm bound
To spend my days
Now ready to atone

———

If pain
Evolves to pleasure
Then why am I
Still awaiting
For this anguish
That afflicts me
Is intense
And unabating

When others are disdainful
Of anxiety I feel
Shocked I cannot just "get better"
And all misery conceal
I grow utterly disheartened
For they surely can't believe
I would ever choose depression
When I'm frantic for reprieve

———

I have but one confession
I'm a victim of depression
Though the world has never guessed
Since the lows are well-repressed
I am overwhelmed with grief
Truly desperate for relief

They say I'll soon "get better"
When I tell them how I feel
How I wish they truly understood
Depression doesn't heal

———

Resistance
And repression
Dredge a channel
To depression

———

I am fearful my own epitaph
And final eulogy
Will reveal I never truly lived
Or left a legacy

I dove headfirst off a mountain
With no thing to brace my fall
And unable to be rescued
Since nobody heard my call

———

My resting place is very low
There's not much further down to go
I'm floundering without a rope
And little will to maintain hope

———

I am drowning
Truly drowning
In a torrent of despair
Yet no one would think
To rescue me
Or take the time to care

I am thrashing
At the bottom
Of a dank, abandoned well
Wondering how
I went from drifting
To submerged in utter hell

———

Who would think our virile bodies
Which ensconce our precious souls
Would abandon us and pass away
Decaying in dank holes

———

My life has been a constant war
To overcome this pain
And so many days it seems to me
My efforts are in vain

If it weren't
For those little faces
Staring up at me
I'd be on
My way to heaven
And contented finally

———

Every day I wonder,
"Should I forge ahead or leave?"
Would my family just continue on
Or take the time to grieve?

———

I've often pondered suicide
And if they'd suffer when I died
Just who would feel the greatest guilt
That stronger bonds were never built
And who would question day and night
"Why didn't I possess foresight?"
And just how much time would it take
Until their sorrow and heartache
Were not so piercing anymore
And life continued as before...

I am hopeful
Ever hopeful
I am living in a dream
And this unrelenting
Terror isn't
All that it would seem
And one day
When I awaken
I will surely come to find
That the bars
Holding me captive
Are erected in my mind

—

I yearn to scamper fearlessly
At whim to laugh and shout
If the prison guard on duty
Would agree to let me out

My brain's a cunning tyrant
And my thoughts a well-armed foe
Boldly taunting even while I sleep
Refusing to let go
They advise me "don't trust others"
And forewarn "take extra care"
Then admonish "do keep quiet,
Never show your deep despair"
They inflame my heart with anger
That propels me to my knees
As I plainly beg for mercy
Though unable to appease
Yet I'm ready to start living
Not reacting out of fear
How I wish they both would step aside
And let soul lead from here

How can I love
Or learn to trust
When all I know
Will turn to dust?

———

Who were you as a child
Before you buckled to convention
Grew enshrouded in pretension
And renounced a life beguiled?

———

When did we become so small
Embarrassed to be seen at all
Content to just believe the lies
Rejecting our soul's poignant cries
And never living joyfully
Expressing who we're meant to be?

The mind craves formulations
Shifting truths to fixed designs
For it's never satiated
Living absent rigid lines

———

A rigidity of thinking
Leaves us timid and confined
Never gaining absolution
Since a soul is not defined

———

No problems can exist
That our minds did not create
With its hopes, fears and desires
And intent to forestall fate

It's time to close my eyes
Beneath this blanket of despair
For the unrelenting darkness
Is much more than I can bear

———

If the point
Of my existence
Doesn't matter
Let me know
For unless
I'm serving purpose
I'd much rather
Just let go

———

I often wish I'd fall asleep
And never wake again
Knowing all this pain would vanish
And I'd rest in solace then

Enshrouded by the body
Arrested by the mind
Deluded by the heartache
Abandoned by mankind
Exploited by the senses
Misguided by ego
And just where the madness takes me
I have yet to truly know

———

All division's in the mind
Which in thought forsakes us blind
To what's waiting patiently
And inviting us to be

My body
Needs a respite
From this heavy
Head and heart
Hopeful it
Will find enlightenment
Once they
Are far apart

———

I thought life was so unfair
For quite emphatically believed
That it must meet my presumptions
But left utterly deceived
When it fell short of that vision
With me powerless to sway
What the future had in store
And simply reeling in dismay
Till I came to see such clinging
To a rigid plan or goal
Just impeded me from taking
Risks that truly served my soul

I need to scream and pound my fists
I need a friend to hear
I need to say I'm overwhelmed
With chronic doubt and fear
I need a rock to lean on
I need a way to share
I need to know it's not a lie
When others claim to care
I need to air my feelings
I need to take critique
I need to hold my head up high
Compelled to boldly speak
I need to rest my body
I need to clear my head
I need to go to sleep at night
Awash in peace not dread

I fervently
Implore you
To just give
Me one small sign
That I'm on
A course of promise
Through my action
Or design
For I need to
Know this instant
That the joys
Will trump the pain
And the battle
I am waging
Won't be blindly
Fought in vain
I am fearful
Oh so fearful
If you do
Not show me light
I will lose
The will to live
And choose to end
This futile fight

The ego tells our heart
That we must cast all others out
By denouncing and fault-finding
And consuming us with doubt

———

When our egos do the talking
We grow distanced from our hearts
Leading to misunderstandings
And dissention that imparts

———

Our egos wholly revel
In the trappings of a role
For it offers validation
And illusion of control

———

The ego's only mission
Is to hinder its demise
By concocting tales of fiction
So we're brainwashed by the lies

Why do many choose to lead
Lives miles from their own
Function daily to please others
Spend their years lost and alone
Unaware of where they're headed
Guided by convention's scheme
Forced to banish all emotion
And relinquish every dream
How I wish we had the courage
To commence an insight quest
For it's only through intention
That we'll freely come to rest

My palette carries
Blacks and grays
No vibrant tones
To paint my days
The canvas flush
In muted hues
Arising from
These chronic blues

———

My landscape
Featured brilliant hues
Transformed to toneless grays
With the palette
Now awash in gloom
As darkness paints my days

You think I'm strong
But clearly wrong
For what you really see
Is a lifelong guise
For past these eyes
I'm thrashing helplessly

———

I am struggling
To stay afloat
Since doom and gloom
Have sunk my boat

———

Both life's beauty and its pain
Are so impossible to bear
I'm left basking in elation
Or succumbing to despair

I spend my days suffused in dread
A hostage caged inside my head
Yet venture not beyond these walls
When days extend and nature calls
For riddled so with such despair
And finding not a soul to care
Resolve to live a life confined
Repressing demons in my mind

———

Always churning
Madly yearning
For the peace I long to find
Always sighting
Bent on fighting
Grisly demons in my mind

Why are all thoughts
That fill my head
Of doom and gloom
And death and dread?

———

My head and heart
Are bitter foes
And never will agree
My head and heart
Forge all my woes
And live to torment me

———

Our attachment to the body
Ever bound in time and space
Leaves us utterly restricted
From our own abiding grace

Please hinder the noise
I've lost track of the joys
I can't hear anymore
With this deafening roar
I can't see anymore
With this staggering light
I can't breathe anymore
With this stifling fright

———

I long to live free
Of this despondency
Finding someone to care
That such crushing despair
Leaves me writhing in pain
Sensing all is in vain
Suffocating in fear
With demise looming near

Who will be the victor
In this skirmish having raged
For so long inside my body
As I've fought and greatly aged
Is it Soul completely shattered
Truly longing for relief
Or the Heart crying for mercy
Ever overwhelmed by grief
Is it Brain endlessly churning
Now beseeching for a rest
Or the Dreams yearning to break free
And take flight beyond my chest?

—

There's a battle raging in my head
A full-scale bloody war
With the casualties all mounting
Although violence I abhor
Yet there's no sign of surrender
And I fear no end in sight
Not until my battered being
Can no longer bear the fight

The burden
Of myself
Has grown
Impossible to bear
Although rather
Than slip further
Down this mountain
Of despair
I will simply
Cry for help
And hope an angel
Hears my plea
Or I'll not
Survive much longer
And succumb
To misery

Though the terror lies within us
We can't nullify the mind
That torments us in such ways
We hurt ourselves and act unkind

———

My mind is truly terrified
Of feeling nothingness
So it badgers and torments me
With desires and distress

———

We're so bound by feeling separate
And imprisoned in the mind
We live guided by the ego
Playing roles it has defined

Most every day I wonder
What our lives will come to mean
In the end when death comes calling
Were we ever truly seen?

———

I can't hold my head up high
And just pretend to be okay
I can't wear this phony smile
Throughout another lonely day
I can't bolster those around me
And assure them all is well
When I'm bowing to the pain
With no escaping from this hell

No one has the wherewithal
To take the time and see
That I'm living with depression
And succumbing helplessly

———

Am I really that convincing
Or perhaps they just don't care
For beneath this guise I'm drowning
In an ocean of despair

———

This endless grief
Streaming freely from my soul
Carries no relief
Though I'm desperate to be whole

Time's passage still cannot erase
That vision of her tragic face
With eyes beseeching me to stay
When I preferred to turn away
Now castigated for disdain
I'm bound to bear eternal pain
Since even on my brightest days
I'm always haunted by her gaze

———

When I burst into this world
Awash in curiosity
There was never thought I'd buckle
To profound anxiety
Overshadowing the promise
Once reflected on my face
And supplanting future dreams
With just a shadow in their place

The belief we must "be something"
Is the source of all our pain
In demanding validation
That impounds us in the brain

———

The body may appear to act
Completely on its own
But in truth reflects a mind
And its pretentious needs alone

———

A tune today played in my head
Yet when I turned it quickly fled
Now struggle I to somehow find
What ran so sweetly through my mind
Yet resolution to recall
Yields not a single strain at all
And grief for this lost melody
Will never cease to chastise me

I muster a brave smile to hide
The truth that I am terrified
Of every thing I can't control
Abandoned in a gaping hole
And shoveling like mad to fill
A void that's ever-present still

———

There is nothing more unfortunate
Than rote conformity
For we're shrouded from that higher self
Just yearning to break free

———

A journey without obstacles
Serves no intent at all
For true wisdom isn't gained
Without a fierce, protracted haul

If suffering alone
Was what we needed to grow wise
Then we'd all have found fulfillment
Having faced inclement skies

———

Our greatest superpowers
Are the ones that we deny
Scared to harness their potential
And attempt to truly fly

I have felt your anguish of the soul
With grief that found no end
I have shared your madness of the mind
Unable to transcend
I have braved your isolation
In a world too blind to care
I have suffered through the grief you bore
Encumbered by despair
I have known your meaningless of life
Unsure of why I'm here
Moved to lock myself inside
Incarcerated by the fear
I have burned with your desire
To channel darkness into light
Truly desperate for creation
To move others with insight
Wholly certain such intent to morph
Sheer pain to vibrant art
Just as animate as we
With pure exuberance and heart
Must sustain us through our days
For if we set these treasures free
They'll illuminate the world
To let us shine eternally

What were your parting thoughts
As you renounced your futile fight
Did you wonder if the ones back home
Would ever sleep at night?
Did you question if tomorrow
Might dawn better than today
Thus repent this crushing act
Contrived to take the pain away?
Did you ponder other options
To departing mortal life
Seeking reasons to keep fighting
And make meaning of the strife?
Did you trust it would be easier
To never feel again
Than wrest beauty from the chaos
And perhaps find solace then?

I've spent my life a loner
On the outside looking in
Fighting unrelenting demons
Which antagonized within

———

I am suffering in silence
So the world will never see
All this anguish wholly shrouded
Yet still terrorizing me

———

Worry serves no purpose
And impounds us in the head
Fearing what may never happen
Yet left wallowing in dread

———

Captive in the trance of thinking
Keeps us separate and small
Disconnected from our hearts
And never living life at all

For years I thought outsiders
Left me shackled in a cage
But in truth it was my head
That held me captive by the rage

————

Dependence on some one or thing
To bring us happiness
Leads to misery and heartache
For it hinges on success

————

Our relentless search for pleasure
Is the source of all our pain
For a hostage to desire
Leaves us shackled by the brain

————

Passion instigates the mind
For desire makes us blind
To the love that's free of pain
Deep within the heart not brain

How amazing that the mind
Can turn a moment of sheer bliss
Into harrowing despair
Once it succumbs to hopelessness

———

Though I'm terrified of leaving
Real epiphanies unstated
Nature's marvels undetected
Or art unappreciated
Fate will dawn with countless gifts
Remaining utterly unknown
And accepting that as truth
Will take a lifetime to condone

You will never see another
Winter soften into spring
When the landscape is reborn
And birds return to gaily sing
Or gaze spellbound as the dark of night
Gives way to breaking dawn
Or anticipate a rainstorm
Snug in bed with curtains drawn
Or luxuriate affront a fire
On winter's coldest days
Or enjoy a sweet tomato
Ripened by the sun's warm rays
Or inhale the smell of lavender
Transported on the breeze
Or find solace as the wind
Serenely rustles through the trees
You will never share another
Peal of laughter with a friend
For the world in all its beauty
Couldn't save you in the end

PERFECTIONISM AND MARTYRDOM

My earliest truth was that I could never achieve
perfection in my parents' eyes. No matter how intently
I labored to be the quintessential daughter or how
well I performed, they always seemed disappointed,
neglecting to see me as caring and characterizing
me as selfish and unkind. However, being so fearful
of provoking further anger or disapproval, I never
showed irritation or stood up for myself, ever striving
to avoid confrontation and maintain peace. Since
when an angry parent is happy, life is manageable and
everyday existence relatively stable. But the minute
a volcano started smouldering with the telltale signs
I knew too well—the furrowed brow, the caustic
scowl, the heaviness of a step ascending or descending
stairs and the slamming of doors—the terror of, *"it's
happening"* would suffuse me in all-engulfing panic. I
therefore lived each day petrified of possible eruption,
knowing its potential for devastation and convinced
I must remain faultless to prevent displeasure and
earn validation. And all the while, I was certain our
household dysfunction was entirely *"my fault"* and
bore full responsibility to *"fix everyone and everything."*
Yet since those closest to me only saw me as flawed,
that was ultimately how I came to see myself as well,
despising the person I was and desperately trying to be
someone else.

Becoming a *"pleaser"* to avoid inciting anger originated
with my immediate family members, but eventually
extended to everyone in my life. I was on a rabid

mission to perform however needed to satisfy, delivering whatever asked of me with no outward complaints no matter how I felt or what I'd rather be doing. Since in the few childhood instances I had tentatively said "*no*" or showed any sign of dissention I had been rejected, scorned and given the silent treatment for weeks at a time, left wondering what I could have ever done so wrong. And before long suppressing negative emotion and exhibiting displeasure through the silent treatment became our household method of communication. Whenever one of us felt hurt, we would sullenly ignore the perpetrator rather than express our anger verbally. These stand-offs never ended in actual reconciliations; instead, after weeks of silence we'd gradually relent and resume our normal pattern of interaction as if nothing had ever happened. Yet at no time were feelings or events instigating these long silences discussed, apologies given for indignities hurled in anger, or admission of responsibility for wrongdoing expressed. I thus always felt guilty for creating unrest I didn't understand the derivation of, and was left perplexed over being deemed a culprit without any logical explanation for why.

I soon came to believe I could only exhibit positive feelings, since they alone would maintain peace and prevent unrest. Negative feelings were to be suppressed as they incited agitation. This also meant I must mask all adversity since I couldn't risk others hearing news with potential to dismay or infuriate.

Ultimately this act of suppressing contrary opinion and honest expression shaped my personality, turning me into a martyr unable to develop healthy relationships and creating a deep, simmering resentment permeating my entire being.

My desire to please manifested in an all-out mission to attain perfection in both my appearance and pursuits. For starters, my body needed to mirror those of females I aspired to become and befriend—tall, slender, and perfectly proportioned, with long, tanned legs and impeccable features. I wanted my skin to be radiant, eyes translucent blue, and effortlessly toss flowing, wavy, naturally blond tresses, plus the confident way in which I carried myself, smiled and conversed to turn heads and ingratiate all. Being in such denial of who I was and so intent on being everything I was not, I became maniacally focused on fulfilling an unattainable vision. Let's be clear, this wasn't just a lofty dream but a fanatical mission to emulate and gain acceptance from the most popular individuals with whom I shared not one thing in common. For in truth, I was petite and brunette with acne-prone skin, short, stocky legs and a flat chest. And in personality I was awkward, forced, insecure and terrified of speaking to strangers—a churning, heady, intense, overly-sensitive, repressed creative. Nothing was effortless for me since all human interactions were terrifying ordeals in which I came across forced, stilted and as if I was trying too hard to appear likeable and at ease. Nonetheless, all actions and behaviors were externally directed toward creating a facade hinging on performance and superficial appearance.

Not only did my bodily appearance disgust me, but its physical frailty was continually threatening betrayal as well. I believed my body must perform flawlessly and prove impervious to damaging infiltrators—the pinnacle of perfection and entirely immune to sickness, hormones, emotions and aging. Aches, disease, sagging, wrinkles and malaise signified weakness and the march toward destiny, and I refused to face the same fate as other mere mortals. I thus determined to control all inputs entering my "*temple*" to ensure it remained free of poisons and toxins, while also keeping it in continual motion to avoid remaining sedentary and spreading, settling, expanding, aging and decaying. Any physical weakness was to be denied or masked at all cost. In fact, even as a young child I would hide all sickness and actually run the thermometer under *cold* water to negate my fever and attend school, certain teachers would see me as imperfect if I missed even one day. To be ill, tired, angry and distraught were weaknesses with potential to magnify deficiency and elicit pity, disapproval or criticism. For even when I masked fallibility, others still found fault with me, so the implications of actually revealing shortcomings were unfathomable. I therefore swallowed all foible and emotion, vowing to conceal any mistake, sickness, pain, displeasure or discomfort from the world. And acting in such manner inevitably rendered me unaware of what was normal for humans to experience and feel.

While on the one extreme I obsessed over *"perfect human specimens"* determined to mimic them, on the other I was appalled by the vast majority of those who were flawed. These loafers didn't care one bit about abusing themselves—ingesting poisons, idling and ultimately carrying so much extra flesh it exhausted and weakened their bodies leading to a host of lifestyle-based diseases and conditions. I needed to be housed in a container looking both perfect on the outside and immune to harmful intruders on the inside. In fact, all I cared about were the necessary actions to prevent aging and achieve immortality. Yet as much as I engaged in every imaginable precaution, I still suffered the same vulnerabilities as ordinary humans, a truth quite difficult to accept.

In addition to putting intense pressure on myself to achieve perfection physically and socially, I also believed I must attain academic excellence, with any grade lower than 100% unacceptable. Since I never learned failure was an essential part of life and necessary to building confidence and wisdom, I didn't view it as beneficial in any sense. I rather became defined by achievement alone, and when ultimately falling short of my outsized expectations I shattered, believing myself insignificant and unworthy if not perfect. I viewed failure as permanent and ending my future—unable

to see life beyond fallibility. Eventually this obsessive perfectionism became the essence of who I was as a person. To be acceptable to myself—which meant maintaining self-respect and a sense of security—I needed to attain exemplary outcomes with continual success. It was either black or white; in my warped view, anything short of A+ was *failure*, with 100 *perfect* and 99 *imperfect*. In fact, I adopted that mindset very early on; even my first grade teacher predicted trouble later in life. *"Melissa is a perfectionist,"* she told my parents, *"and must be number one. She is going to have a very difficult time accepting failure."* She went on to explain I couldn't tolerate making mistakes, becoming hysterical upon learning I had answered a question incorrectly. And this was at age five...

Because of needing to maintain both harmony and perfection at all costs, I turned to chronic lying at a very young age. Any failure or misstep was changed into a positive, denied, or never expressed in order to maintain a flawless front. Yet never once did I question whether my actions were right or wrong, having no realistic sense for what was proper conduct but simply what would maintain peace and garner approval. In fact, whenever I performed poorly on a test, I would concoct fictitious stories for my teachers about an ill mother requiring assistance with medical treatments, long lost relatives visiting and not being able to study, strange illnesses of my own, and needing to console

*To be acceptable
to myself—which
meant maintaining
self-respect and a
sense of security—
I needed to
attain exemplary
outcomes with
continual success.*

my special needs brother, tearfully begging them to allow a retake or provide extra credit assignments to boost my grade. I was literally so determined to spark empathy that I articulated my pleas with compelling, heart-wrenching performances, continually garnering their compassion and support.

I ultimately invented so much of what I was desperate to believe that the line between honesty and dishonesty became blurred. It didn't matter if my actions were deceitful, since I was entirely blind to the how and why and solely focused on the result. Sadly, never once in all those years did I feel guilty about lying to and deceiving others, as my actions were absolutely necessary for survival and continued high-level performance. Wrong to me was appearing imperfect and potentially facing someone's wrath. Thus no one ever knew just how many times I unsuccessfully tried out for musical groups, ran for office and lost, or did poorly on tests, since I never disclosed results. And when there was no choice but to reveal outcomes I simply lied...or blamed my *"failures"* on circumstances beyond my control. This desire for perfection soon superseded all morals; I was on a higher mission in doing whatever it took to win, as the addiction to stellar performance made achievement paramount to everything else. I needed to *"be the best,"* intent on separating myself and winning approval from family and peers. Yet no matter how well I performed, I was still viewed by those closest to me as *"selfish and no good."* Being unfairly blamed for actions that weren't my fault and inaccurately seen and judged by my parents made me horribly defensive to criticism and ever feel victimized, certain *"life wasn't fair,"* with each negative comment a knife stabbing through me. I continually lamented, *"What did I do wrong?"* and was left indignantly perplexed, because I intellectually knew I hadn't done *anything* wrong, yet ended up being blamed nonetheless. After all, I truly wasn't a terrible person, yet my parents were always displeased which made me ever question what I could have done to disappoint them. This eventually developed into a vendetta against the world as I embarked on proving I was a good person and not the transgressor I was depicted to be.

My bitterness at being the victim grew with each passing year, to the point where I became incredibly vengeful when sensing anyone was taking advantage of or blaming me unfairly. In fact, as I aged it induced pure rage, settling into an immense weight on my shoulders sinking me lower and lower. I couldn't seem to let go of the anger once it unleashed, which ultimately channeled into a deep, dark cavern of bitterness. I would continually churn events around and around in my head, analyzing, churning and asking myself over and over, *"Why would they take advantage of me?"* or *"I can't believe they think I'm so stupid,"* with my anger mounting. I could never see past myself long enough to understand others' motives, left questioning, *"Why don't they care about me, why don't they respect me, why do they hate me?"* as opposed to detecting external reasons for their actions. I just took everything so literally and personally, feeling utterly persecuted. I truly didn't want to care so deeply about others' reactions and become weak and defensive, yet had no idea how to diffuse anger and express such overwhelming emotions now festering to the point of explosion. The few times I vented my honest feelings had ended in disaster, so I was petrified of rocking the boat by overreacting and saying something I'd regret. For then I'd be blamed, disdained and left saddled with guilt which was the worst punishment of all.

This devastating sense that others didn't love, understand or care about my feelings made me feel terribly used. Others clearly viewed me as simply a tool to exploit then discard, not only in making me the scapegoat for infrac-tions I didn't commit, but also in holding me hostage to fulfill their personal needs. In my own home, I was just a receptacle for others to continually vent their gripes, never actually hearing me but simply nodding their heads vacuously, oblivious to what I was saying. They asked the seemingly appropriate questions, but barely waited to hear my answers before reverting back to themselves. Then they could ramble for hours with little awareness or concern for how it was impacting me, never bothering to show empathy for who I was since their focus was self-directed.

By my teenage years I had become so emotionally scarred that I no longer trusted people and their motives,

I had no idea how to diffuse anger and express such overwhelming emotions now festering to the point of explosion.

profoundly battered from a lifetime of betrayal. This led me to develop a scathing view toward humanity, which was: if push ever came to shove (which it generally did), humans would act in their best interest to come out on top, even if it hurt others. It was no doubt an ugly way of thinking, but it was entirely honest and my truth. For even if people had good intentions, they invariably became clouded in situations threatening them personally. And if not circumstantially, most just couldn't see beyond their selfish fears and desires to wholly care about anyone else. Yet although I knew others didn't have my best interests at heart and thus despised them, I simultaneously felt tremendous guilt in letting them down. As I aged, this burden of guilt became a chain around my neck dragging me further into despair, second-guessing every move and wondering if I should have acted or thought differently. Having never developed a moral or emotional compass to guide my decision-making, I couldn't access my feelings and was terrified of being wrong or displeasing, which left me wallowing in continual remorse. No matter where I was or what I was doing, I envisioned my parents chastising, *"You are so selfish and only care about yourself."* But why wasn't anyone standing up for me? Why didn't anyone care about *my* feelings? I wanted nothing more than to break free from this prison of guilt, but completely lacked fortitude to do so.

This was an entry from my teenage journal: *"Thank goodness I've never been under the illusion I'll be cared for, loved for who I truly am, or that my dreams will come true* if I wish upon a star since life has hardened me too much for that. In fact, I've been so calloused by life's experiences, disappointments and rejections I've given up expectations of anyone or anything. I can no longer depend on external forces for support or will just be let down and angry at myself for trusting. So I've dug deep and gone it alone. This has brought me to the point where I have little need for anything from anyone—just a castaway on a desert island with merely my thoughts to keep me company. Now if my thoughts were good it might be peaceful on my island. But they are not. For although I have no expectations of those around me, I have unattainable expectations for myself and continually fall short of my personal goals. Mostly, this comes down to playing the role of sister and daughter. Let's be honest, I have failed dismally at both, and despite being a fighter of the greatest proportions am ready to surrender. No matter what I do it is met with derision. Inside, I'm livid and want to scream, 'How dare you look at me with disgust when you are far from flawless yourself!' These people should feel grateful having someone selfless enough to sacrifice her soul for their happiness. But people like this don't care about others' feelings, because when everything is primarily about them nothing a selfless person gives is ever enough. They just suck the life right out of them and keep searching for others to chew up and spit out to better serve their needs. I might as well give up while I still have a little life left in me. Since even when I give it my all, which I have always done, nothing ever changes in their minds. I am still one incident away from scum."

My entire life had been focused on pleasing, pushing my own needs deep below the surface in the act of servitude.

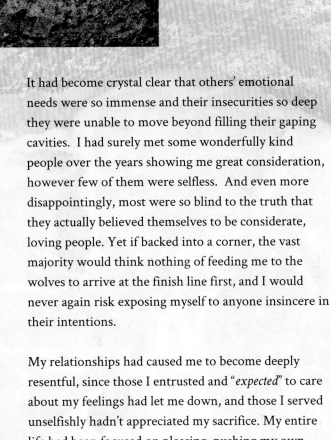

It had become crystal clear that others' emotional
needs were so immense and their insecurities so deep
they were unable to move beyond filling their gaping
cavities. I had surely met some wonderfully kind
people over the years showing me great consideration,
however few of them were selfless. And even more
disappointingly, most were so blind to the truth that
they actually believed themselves to be considerate,
loving people. Yet if backed into a corner, the vast
majority would think nothing of feeding me to the
wolves to arrive at the finish line first, and I would
never again risk exposing myself to anyone insincere in
their intentions.

My relationships had caused me to become deeply
resentful, since those I entrusted and "*expected*" to care
about my feelings had let me down, and those I served
unselfishly hadn't appreciated my sacrifice. My entire
life had been focused on pleasing, pushing my own
needs deep below the surface in the act of servitude.
And although I never believed I would be put on a
pedestal for this sacrifice, I did ultimately presume I
would be appreciated and able to confidently check
the box: "*served my parents and family admirably and
received their gratitude.*" But when others' reactions
weren't validating, my devastation ultimately channeled
into bitter resentment, for the way the world was
"*supposed*" to work had gone awry. I couldn't come to
terms with such unfair treatment, believing if I acted
appropriately and gave as genuinely as possible I would

be rewarded and bask in the glow of gratitude. After
all, that was the law of reciprocity and I had battled to
earn that recognition. But events didn't play out in such
manner since others' selfishness caused them to become
ungrateful, unsatisfied, unfulfilled and unhappy I wasn't
able to give even more than I was ever capable of giving.

This overwhelming sense of injustice *"life wasn't fair"*
plagued me even into my adult life and parenthood
itself. My bitterness over being a doormat was a
simmering pot of water always on the verge of boiling
over. When I generously served others they were
reasonably content, but if I wasn't beckoning with open
arms to satisfy every need, they conveyed displeasure
and demanded compliance. I felt victimized, exploited,
and in a very gray place of no longer wanting to
continue in this manner, yet finding it nearly impossible
to break free. I was well aware that if I spoke up for the
first time without steadfastly serving, I'd be met with
extreme disapproval. And that, needless to say, would
incite tremendous guilt which I was terrified of carrying.

My ultimate realization, however, was a horrifying
personal condemnation. For although I had always
believed myself to be acting unselfishly in steadfastly
serving, I was actually doing so in order to receive
validation, and left terribly disillusioned when rejected.
That made me a martyr—sacrificing my own needs
and perpetually giving, expecting too much and then
disappointed by others' actual behavior. And I was now

at a complete loss on how to handle the magnitude
of that knowledge, reveling in the gravity I had
wasted my entire life trying to please when no one
had ended up pleased or fulfilled at all. My children
and family members were still as needy as ever, never
fully satisfied by what I gave and ever wanting more
despite continual servitude, while I was absolutely
exhausted and miserable from overextending while
denying my own needs. The truth was now crystal
clear: I had wasted my life for nothing in return. It was
a deep, gaping wound piercing my soul and carrying a
profound sense of isolation, meaninglessness and
strong contention that there was no point in even
trying, since my efforts were in vain. People only
cared about themselves and I was nothing but
a worthless pawn. The old demons were back, and I
could hardly raise my head off the pillow since life was
absolutely futile.

However, I finally came to see that in blindly serving
everyone I was actually serving no one, with only
myself to blame if not communicating my needs. For if
I continually served without belief I deserved to be
seen as something more, then I couldn't expect others
to see me as anything more. That robotic, emotionless
servant who never said a word and just mindlessly
completed tasks wasn't my true self but a puppet who
would never find solace or succor. In fact, as I reflected
on my life, I realized that ruthless inner tyrant had
never given me permission to just stop and breathe,

In order to find salvation it was essential to respect my needs, express my honest feelings, and wholly manifest my heartfelt truth.

and I could no longer recklessly run myself into the ground without cessation or mercy. In fact, martyrdom now made me feel I was flagrantly betraying my soul, while also disabling family members from building skills necessary to cope and become self-sufficient adults. By continually solving problems my children could easily solve themselves, I was doing them a disservice, delaying their ability to take responsibility for their lives, develop initiative and cultivate fortitude. Thus for everyone's sake, I needed to believe a different truth about what constituted good and bad, becoming confident that saying "*no*" didn't mean I was a terrible person and should feel guilty. It was also critical to accept some inevitable resistance from others, but push through to grant ultimate liberation for all. It was definitely much easier said than done, but in order to find salvation it was essential to respect my needs, express my honest feelings, and wholly manifest my heartfelt truth.

I often stop and ask myself
What have I done so wrong
Unsure why they criticize me
Though I follow right along
And endeavor to please all of them
Perceived as kind and good
Never raise my voice or grumble
Though perhaps I sometimes should
I'm the one who's always there to give
A smile or warm embrace
And treat others with compassion
That delivers hope and grace
And yet everyone's still beckoning
Demanding I give more
And I'm left forever wondering
Just what they're searching for

I disagree with what you say
Yet feign approval anyway
For pleasers learn to nod and smile
And keep their feelings in denial

———

I have found remaining silent
Without uttering a word
Is preferred to boldly speaking out
And never being heard

———

If we only bolster others
And neglect to serve the self
We'll forever leave our dreams
Collecting dust upon a shelf

I'm surrounded by such narcissists
And function as a tool
Serving everyone who beckons
Then discarded like a fool

———

When we prostrate to their wishes
And accept our destiny
We relinquish any chance
To impact what is yet to be

I long to
Share my struggles
And I yearn to
Voice my fears
But I'm older now
With efforts spent
On drying
Others' tears

———

Expectation
Fuels distress
With fervent need
To reach success
And constant pressure
To achieve
Once preconditioned
To believe
That when we fail
And face defeat
Our lives will never
Be complete

I'm not sure the reason why
I feel such a need to lie
But the moment I've told one
I have only just begun
As I'm bound to utter more
Though deception I abhor
Now to those whom I admire
I've become a loathsome liar

———

When they told me to stop crying
And assume a happy face
I grew focused on complying
For I couldn't bare a trace
Of the anguish that endured
Beneath a well-established guise
Yet condemned to live inured
From a persona built on lies

Though I tell myself
I shouldn't care
What others think or say
In reality
I'm desperate for
Their praise to feel okay

—

When you disregard my feelings
Acting callous, rude and mean
I feel utterly rejected
And entirely unseen

Too oft I give
Without receiving
And though intent
On still believing
Kindness I
Bestow today
Will down the road
Come back my way
To be acknowledged
Would be nice
And even once
Perhaps suffice

I dry their tears
Erase their fears
And answer every plea
Although when I fall
And meekly call
Nobody rescues me

———

I'm tired of putting others' needs
Above my very own
When I'm unappreciated
For the selflessness I've shown
Which suffuses me in rancor
That I'm never truly seen
Just a weak, defenseless servant
Wholly shackled by routine

They assert their endless orders
With continual critique
Though I'm desperate to be other
Than a servant scared to speak

———

They ask me how
I think they look
Most each and every day
And yet all the while
They preen themselves
I'm withering away

———

Please help me
Truly help me
To continue down my path
For so many
Aim to fell me
With the venom of their wrath

The words you
Hurled to punish
Did instead help set me free
At last ready
To relinquish
This responsibility
As I've labored
Ever humbly
To oblige your every need
Yet you chose to slash
The hand that gave
Content to watch it bleed
So I leave you
On this journey
With no wisdom, warmth or pride
Just the hope
Compassion finds you
And bestows a steadfast guide

They're all clinging to my feathers
And I'm struggling to fly
From the strain of ever serving
Obligated to comply
Yet I'm promptly growing weaker
And I know it won't be long
Till I buckle from this burden
For I'm really not that strong

———

If we pander to the crowd
As just a deferential sheep
Bound to heed affirmed opinions
Without uttering a peep
We will never find the strength
To blaze our own transcendent path
Unconcerned with what's ahead
Or their anticipated wrath

They were bigger
Louder, bolder
Unforgiving
Rash and strong
I was timid
Bent on pleasing
And just blindly
Went along
And before I
Even knew it
I surrendered
Heart and soul
And became
A mindless servant
Though I truly
Loathed the role

They were needy
And convincing
So dissenting
Just seemed wrong
I was desperate
For approval
And compelled
To go along
Then without a
Moment's notice
I was simply
Swallowed whole
Living fully
Isolated
From my
Empathetic soul

I betrayed my soul for decades
To serve others in my life
So convinced their recognition
Would allay the inner strife
But it turns out I pleased no one
As we all were seeking more
When I should have focused inwardly
And taught myself to soar

———

I relinquished independence
To help others bear life's strain
Left my selfhood in a cavern
Certain sainthood I'd attain
Yet despite such ardent efforts
To fulfill their every need
I was utterly forsaken
For a martyr's never freed

I'm exhausted from commitment
And responsibility
With the strain of serving others
Yet aspiring to run free
I'm distressed from hiding who I am
Crouched deep inside a shell
Truly desperate to express myself
And circumvent this hell

———

When we're shackled to performance
Chasing calculated goals
We stay captive in our heads
And disconnected from our souls

———

If all our learned behavior
Is directed outwardly
With a sense of worth derived
From needing constant flattery
We will never feel impelled
To access who we truly are
And allow that inner fire
To become our guiding star

Though some surely may be lazy
Most are terrified of trying
For the fear of falling short
Supplants the thrill of boldly vying

———

Searching outside for the light
That can be only found within
Leaves us distanced from our souls
Where introspection must begin

———

If we spend our days assessing
Why folks do the things they do
We'll neglect to gaze within
And ascertain what rings most true

———

I'm consumed with the sense
That my life isn't fair
And all others are vain
Though pretending to care

I'll never trust
I'm on my own
For all examples
I've been shown
Find those who boldly
Claim to care
Are selfish
And that isn't fair

———

I spent decades waiting meekly
For the world to grant me praise
Certain armed with validation
I would rise above the haze
Yet when cheers were not forthcoming
Grew resentful and cast blame
Well aware that I was only
A blank face without a name
So I summoned my lost courage
With intention quite sincere
To release all expectation
Choosing love to vanquish fear

I don't care about the process
I'm just focused on the goal
For it's only flush in victory
I'm able to feel whole

———

As long as I'm imperfect
I will find it hard to rest
Still relentlessly pursuing
This compulsion to be best

———

I'm not here to access knowledge
Just to garner perfect grades
For it's only in achievement
That my desperation fades

We mustn't let the unlived dreams
Of others fill our head
But endeavor to reveal
Our soul's authentic cry instead

———

I was tethered to the outcome
With success the central goal
Left imprisoned by cognition
And restricted from my soul

———

If only we adored
Our truest selves right from the start
We would cherish every quirk
Instead of tearing them apart

If tomorrow was the last time
You would bid me a goodbye
Would you offer an apology
Or explanation why
Our repeated interactions
Sparked unfortunate attacks
And continual rejection
Of support and loving acts?
Would you survey me disdainfully
As if I'd lost my mind
Or now choose to grant forgiveness
Casting prior ills behind?

—

Though I'm terribly disheartened
By the barbs you hurl my way
I still live my life intent
On finding promise every day

I don't need a show of feigned remorse
For what was wrongly said
But would rather you endeavor
To act differently instead

———

How do you help that someone
Who would rather just complain
Than wholeheartedly endeavor
To wrest meaning from their pain?

———

If we ever feed the ego
We will truly starve the soul
For pursuing validation
Cannot ever make us whole

I can weather my own anguish
But can't bear another's grief
For I feel I've surely failed
When helpless to impart relief

———

My well is dry
I have no more
And even if
The rain should pour
A hole this deep
Would slowly fill
And leave a
Gaping chasm still

———

I can hardly stand the burden
Of my own profound despair
But when coupled with my children's
Is impossible to bear

When at last we disengage
From the opinions of our peers
We'll be free to live our lives
No longer hostage to our fears

———

We all pray at many altars
But must choose to honor one
For unless we serve the self
Our woes have only just begun

I have always viewed their selfishness
Much too offensively
Since in truth I know they aren't
Really trying to hurt me
But so focused on themselves
They're blind to every other thing
And unable to show mercy
For the pain their actions bring

———

Though I'm utterly disheartened
By what others do and say
And feel deeply disappointed
By their penchant to betray
I must not allow contempt
To cruelly devastate my soul
Rather morph this desolation
Into actions I control

THE FUTILE RACE

Even at a very
young age I somehow
knew the painful
reality of existence
that we would
all die, we were
fundamentally alone,
and no one would
ever know the real us.

Even at a very young age I somehow knew the painful reality of existence that we would all die, we were fundamentally alone, and no one would ever know the real us. In essence, there was no inherent meaning or value to life. This burden of mortality was so overwhelming I yearned for nothing more than to escape beyond myself to a world where peace reigned supreme and the existential noise subsided. Yet unable to empty my head, I grappled with a profound sense of *"not quite rightness,"* and urgency to act and do *"something"* to quiet the clamor, helpless as the clock ticked away to my impending demise.

If I allowed the reality of destiny to surface, the futility of existence became all-consuming with my fate imminent and darkness ever-looming. Despite my words or actions, I was doomed with no salvation in this foolish quest for immortality. And yet, no one else seemed to have gotten the memo. *Why didn't others realize life was fleeting, and if they did, why didn't they care?* All I ever thought about was how quickly years were passing and needing more precious time, while everyone else squandered time like it meant absolutely nothing. It was as if I was looking at the world wearing augmented reality glasses, and although I desperately wished to flee the dungeon of my mind and find solace, I was actually powerless to affect anything at all.

A large portion of this unsettledness stemmed from the fact my internal engine was super-charged and

on overdrive. I was literally so *"wired"* that my hands
would shake quite noticeably if held straight out in
front of me, which felt horribly disconcerting and
as if my body was careening out of control. But the
awareness of racing was most pronounced when I
became inactive or bored in any manner. Being quiet
or still made the drumbeat of mortality overwhelmingly
loud and impelled perpetual motion to stem the
unease—getting up, getting out and keeping continually
busy to quell this overwhelming sense of dread.
With such urgent need to create form from chaos I
developed a host of nervous habits enabling me to
remain sedentary when forced to sit still, like obsessive
nail and lip biting, fixation on removing split ends
from my hair and compulsive picking at my cuticles
and face as well. Because focusing on these specific
behaviors eased panic and diverted my attention from
physical activity. This agitation also made periods
of silence unbearable with an urgent desire to speak
and fill all conversation voids. I couldn't tolerate my
inability to control the direction a discussion would
take, envisioning others criticizing me or thinking I
was unacceptably dull during any hush. I was thus
compelled to keep rambling, either telling a nonstop
flurry of prepared jokes or anecdotes contrived for
particular situations, or more commonly asking a
steady stream of questions to engage others and keep
the exchange flowing smoothly.

Since helpless to transcend this circumstantial powerlessness, I instead grabbed hold of whichever of my own actions I could affect to feel a semblance of control. Everything else was too ephemeral and impossible to impact, explaining why I became terribly obsessed with academic performance early in life. Achievement was the one area that delivered the control and validation I desperately craved, as I was able to perform at a high level and set myself apart in attaining tangible results from my efforts. It's therefore no wonder I began placing increased emphasis on the outcome of my endeavors as I matured. I needed to know the harder I worked, the better performance or greater success I would attain. And if the end justified the means and I received recognition for my effort, I remained content and could rest relatively easily.

This fervent need to exert control over my daily behavior, given destiny was immutable, also extended to food intake, exercise level and spending. And most unfortunately, it was demonstrated in a very punishing, all-or-nothing manner. I truly reveled in the power of depriving myself through starvation, over-exercising, demanding A-pluses and stinginess as I was able to see immediate results directly appear on a scale, in muscle definition, on a test or in my wallet. I inevitably became addicted to that sense of control, having never felt it in other aspects of life.

Although I used many metaphors for behaving like a marionette with others (or the universe) manipulating my strings, water and the ocean were most fitting for what I was experiencing inwardly. It seemed as if I was either drowning or being dragged against my will by the current and continually battered against the shore, powerless to ease the pummeling. And instead of relaxing into the current, I aggressively fought back against it. I now realize this mirrored the way I dealt with any uncomfortable emotion—denying, submerging and resisting when I actually needed to let those feelings engulf me as I ideally would have done with a strong current as well. Ultimately, the fear of those feelings triggering resistance was much more destructive than experiencing the feelings themselves.

This ever-present state of unsettledness impelled me to create a very specific plan of action in order to survive each day. I needed to orchestrate every moment of free time, looking ahead to the future and anticipating what was coming or unbearable panic would threaten to suffocate me. An ideal weekend was therefore jam-packed with activity from the moment I awoke until the moment I climbed into bed thoroughly exhausted, having been in continual motion to successfully avoid the terror of "*nothingness.*" Keeping busy included activities like obsessively running with my children to visit museums and attractions and fill my head with marvelous sights, engaging in multitudes of research projects in retail stores to study juvenile products, and an obsession with coupon clipping and bargain hunting. I had become quite a hoarder and knew it was indeed an addiction, for I truly loved the thrill of finding underpriced treasures, acquiring brand-name clothing at ridiculously low prices, or purchasing beautiful, handmade trinkets and crafts intoxicating my senses. I had piles of unused items now filling multiple closets, since I desperately craved tangible baubles to marvel at and hold precious when life was fleeting, and collecting trifles gave the illusion I was connecting to meaningful objects grounded in reality. However, purchasing ultimately became an unhealthy method of transcending chemicals and thoughts raging unchecked through my body, as I basked in the adrenaline surge of finding that illusive needle in the haystack.

This need for motion also manifested itself in actual exercise, growing obsessed with the continual movement of my limbs. Exercising filled my relentless desire to gain control of the uncontrollable through: 1) becoming the pinnacle of health and protecting my body against disease to forestall death, 2) controlling my weight and appearing more like the girls I wished to emulate, and 3) avoiding the dark thoughts pummeling my head through pushing my body to new levels and achieving physical goals. I exercised nearly every waking moment, even running in place when seated at the table for a meal or working at my desk. This ultimately became a rabid addiction and entirely subconscious, as I innately used motion to ease the existential angst that plagued me.

This fervent urge to keep moving, coupled with the
fear of never missing out on any experience or event
was constant and followed me throughout my teenage
years even into adult life and parenthood. I was truly
petrified that if not physically present with my peers
or family, something memorable would happen and I'd
miss out on the experience. It was an all-out panicky
feeling of needing to be in attendance at all costs,
although I didn't even quite know why. As a child if I
missed an event others were attending I would remain
paralyzed for the entire length of the activity, counting
the minutes until they were home and nothing else
notable could take place in my absence. I would
literally pray on bended knee that nothing life-changing
was occurring without me, for I couldn't bear to be left
out of any transformative experience.

Even as a parent I believed I must, under all circumstances, be present at every single one of my children's
activities. I couldn't miss a minute of anything—whether
it was a game, concert, field trip or celebration—so fearful
that a pivotal moment would occur in my absence.
Ultimately that fear became a terrible pressure nearly
suffocating me, as I had numerous children with overlap-
ping activities and couldn't physically attend all of them.
I was therefore forced to choose which events to attend,
proving even more stressful than needing to attend all
of them in the first place. Since if I chose incorrectly and
missed out on that one unforgettable experience, I would
forever feel guilty with no one to blame but myself.

For some reason, I also never imagined the relentless pressure I felt personally to achieve perfection would extend in the same manner to my children. Of course I wasn't aware of this latent urge as I embarked on motherhood, fearful but with all the best intentions. But perfectionism is ruthless, and without even realizing what was happening, my fierce competitive nature insidiously kicked in with the need to *"be the best"* encompassing them as well. Suddenly I was feeling horrible performance panic for my children, or maybe it was actually for myself—no longer knowing where I ended and they began. Almost overnight it was imperative for *them* to be the very best athletes, brightest students, and most popular of their peer group to ensure my sense of wholeness. And once again, I had a very difficult time handling *my* devastation when reality fell short of expectations. I certainly put on the same brave front I had worn throughout my early life and never let them or others see the pain it invoked, but my sense of disappointment was overwhelming. As my children grew older, this performance pressure became increasingly difficult to bear, since their failures were becoming more public. Suddenly others were witnessing firsthand when my children failed, and I found that terribly shaming. Now there were awards they weren't winning, honors classes they weren't placed in, bases loaded hits they weren't getting, free throws to win games they weren't making, all-star teams they weren't selected for, intensity and grit they weren't demonstrating, etc. And as much as I fought to change these outcomes and push them to try harder or demand higher levels of achievement, I ultimately had very little control over how they performed, who they were as individuals, and what they truly desired for themselves.

Although I knew my children had intellectual ability to succeed, I couldn't force them to care about their grades and continually study if they didn't value learning. Although they had athletic ability, I couldn't force them to practice more intensely for their specific sports if they preferred hanging out with friends. And even if they spoke passionately about making a difference, I couldn't force them to engage in real world causes and fight for change if they weren't willing to get off the sofa and take action. But the crux of my frustration was I just couldn't tolerate them choosing to be average when they were capable of so much more. And it seemed as if they were content remaining ordinary, when I couldn't understand how anyone could accept staying entrenched in mediocrity rather than striving for number one! What was the point in taking up Earth's precious space if you weren't leaving your mark and making it better than when you entered? Intellectually I knew I should accept my children for who they were, appreciate their individual strengths, and go with the flow, but I couldn't seem to do so in practice. In fact, it had gotten to the point where I wasn't even able to enjoy their activities unless they stood out as exceptional. I needed them to be

unusual, different, special, gifted and set themselves apart from the pack, because if they stood out then I would stand out as well, luxuriating in their glow and feeling superior myself. So in truth, it was actually all about me!

For a short time I became so fixated on my children's performance and how they would match up against their peers I even hesitated attending their sporting events, as the thought of watching them fail on a public stage was just too agonizing. And although my rational self generally won out, I chose to park and *"camp out"* far away from other spectators, since my high level of anxiety made it difficult to mingle. Once again, the goal of all endeavors had become solely about the outcome and achieving a predetermined result. If the result was positive and my children looked impressive, I was happy as a lark and thrilled to engage in social banter, as they had shown themselves superior to their rivals. Yet if they didn't stand out as exemplary, I immediately fell into deep malaise and rapidly exited the premises. It was so extreme, soaring to the heights of victory one moment and then descending to the bowels of despair the next, based entirely on performance. Under no circumstance did I want to feel this way and care about such unimportant metrics in the scheme of life. I truly knew actual performance didn't matter, only wanting my children to enjoy their activities, find their passions and be happy! But I couldn't seem to control the obsessive mania wreaking havoc as it had grown into a massive oak tree with roots spreading throughout my entire being. Growing up, superficial performance was all that mattered and I never placed value on pursuing enriching experiences, nurturing inner qualities, developing new skills, teamwork, or finding true fulfillment. I was now an adult, yet that mindset hadn't changed one iota. But given it now included my children, I had even less control over the outcome, making me more panicked than ever before. And most unfortunately, it was still about me and what I wanted (and needed) from them, not about what they wanted (and needed) for themselves.

In my career as an entrepreneur and product designer this obsessive perfectionism was a difficult curse to transcend as well. The need to be perfect made me incredibly risk-averse and terrified of failure—two of the very qualities I needed to embrace most. The thought of creating a product that might fail was almost unbearable, as it would be magnified on such a public stage. These widespread failures initially stung horribly, since so many of my early introductions were massive bombs. I was utterly mortified that creations emerging directly from me didn't resonate with consumers and were soundly rejected. But I unfortunately had no other means of creating than undergoing that process, since I never knew for certain whether a product would succeed or fail ahead of time. No matter how ardently I endeavored to orchestrate success in advance, I truly didn't know a product's potential until it was placed in the hands of customers. Thus if I wanted to create products I was *"forced,"* you could say, to risk failure and put them into the marketplace again and again, not knowing the result until I was exposed and the process made public. And thankfully, my creative urge was so great I had no choice but to forge ahead, gradually learning there were incredible lessons in the failures leading to significantly greater successes down the road. Not to mention, the creation process itself moved me out of my head where fear, doubt, and insecurity converged, living in my boundless heart where organic creation flowed freely. Now three decades later, there's no question the failures proved the most essential ingredient to innovation, teaching me far more than all the successes combined!

I also felt the ardent need to *"know everything"* by consuming knowledge as well, desperate to absorb as much inspiring content as possible and not miss out on that one profound piece of wisdom with potential to transform my entire life trajectory. Yet as material became increasingly accessible with the proliferation of the internet, Amazon, Netflix, additional channels of cable television and handheld screens, it became ever difficult to manage the overwhelming plethora of available offerings. My age-old feeling of needing to read and watch everything, then effectively process it all to never miss out on a gem able to change my life or give me that one-in-a-million idea, started overwhelming me. However, this obsession was

entirely out of fear rather than authentic desire to ingest
worthy content. In fact, I actually reached a point
where my brain was hemorrhaging from too much
input—nothing was able to distill through it as I was
rabidly reading books, watching series and listening
to successive podcasts at 2x speed to expeditiously
complete and remove them from my unending list.
And although in one sense I enjoyed hearing and
viewing tales of others' profound life experiences,
insights and awakenings, my head was so clogged with
their stories and ideas that I stopped having ideas and
stories of my own. A deluge of information was going
in, yet no more creation coming out. I felt utterly
exhausted and brain-dead, realizing my addiction to
consuming content had completely stifled my outward
creative flow and ability to freely ideate. My life had
become a rabid FOMO and competition to continually
reach the end goal and check boxes off a list rather than
enjoy the journey. However, in reality, it had never
been about experiencing the journey in my heart, since
every pursuit became a ruthless battle in the head and
"must win" contest. Yet that clearly wasn't what my soul
sought because I was still exhausted, tormented and
wholly unfulfilled.

Much of the continual movement necessary to quiet my
engine also manifested itself in the fanatical impulse to
forge tangible products. Although that may not sound
ill-intentioned in statement, the truth is the goal was
primarily focused on quantity not quality. I felt impelled

Now three decades later, there's no question the failures proved the most essential ingredient to innovation, teaching me far more than all the successes combined!

to churn out innumerable verses, songs, crafts, pieces of jewelry, blogs and ultimately thousands of toys in an unending stream, as only incessant output served to mask my relentless malaise. In fact, I would meticulously outline the specific type and number of creations necessary to feel settled on a daily basis: *"Today you are going to create twelve pairs of earrings, two bracelets, three toys and write two verses,"* not stopping until they were plainly displayed before me. And speaking of birthing, my passionate desire to create tangible products even extended to the conception of children, feeling most productive and internally satisfied when pregnant, since birthing children was the most gratifying and effective method of solidifying immortality. I surely would have continued producing additional offspring if my body hadn't been deliberately closed for business by my obstetrician after six C-sections!

This internal drive also made me unbelievably competitive with an all-or-nothing mentality. I unfortunately never did anything *"just for fun."* Because the voices in my head were so raucous, I needed to counter them with an intensity of action even louder and more extreme. And that meant everything I did was with all-out ferocity. There was no pushing halfway down on the gas pedal for me; it was a full-blown contest or not even worth attempting as I needed to be crowned victor, viewing anyone and everyone as my adversary no matter what I was doing or with whom I was doing it. Even if I was walking to a classroom at school, I needed to beat my peers there. If I drew a picture, it needed to be more beautiful than anyone else's, even when there was no comparison. But I was always comparing which was all that mattered, keeping an internal score card and determined to be victorious. Whether I was vying against a true opponent or my own children, relatives or friends, I had to win and strived to do so at all costs, not caring who was left in my wake as long as I reached the finish line first. And although never intellectually understanding that this maniacal racing was to avoid despairing thoughts and drown out the voices in my head questioning life's meaning, I must have subconsciously known slowing down would force me to face the reality of mortality and ensuing disillusionment. I therefore lived life frantically moving from task to task with clearly defined goals leaving no room for thought.

It ultimately became apparent I would never be free until I stopped searching for answers "out there" and found courage to gaze within, finally accepting how and what I was feeling. That was when I literally forced myself to stop running, closed my eyes tightly shut, held my breath, and plunged into the darkness. For the first time ever, I didn't allow myself to run from the existential terror pervading my being. I didn't engage in frenetic activity or positive creation to mask the horror, didn't purchase a shiny object, and didn't endeavor to artificially elevate myself as I had instinctively done in the past. I just simply remained in darkness, although

I still had an urgent need to write verses depicting my feelings exactly as they were. However, I didn't make the result of creating to turn darkness into light, allowing it to stay darkness freely flowing through my heart and out my hand in the same manner it arose in my soul. And I clung so tightly to the anguish, disallowing myself to transcend desolation to find a glimmer of light. I finally needed to experience despair exactly as it was, remaining submerged in its depths with acceptance I might always feel this way. And even thus, I was still on this earth living and breathing in all my horrific brokenness.

Once I experienced the very pit of nothingness I became much less terrified. I had touched mortality in all its bleakness and didn't like it one bit, but now knew exactly how it felt. It was what I had been running from my entire life—fragile, vulnerable me staring meaninglessness in the eye with no weapon but the openness of my soul. Going that low had viciously broken me open, and I was determined to never again let myself race around frenetically to mask those feelings and deny my true essence.

I finally needed to experience despair exactly as it was, remaining submerged in its depths with acceptance I might always feel this way.

My mind is in a constant race
Against a savage foe
Yet at no time hits a finish line
With anything to show
Rather pirouettes incessantly
And every lap it spins
I slip further into madness
Since the tyrant always wins

There's such beauty in this world
That goes entirely unseen
When we're caught in endless doing
And imprisoned by routine

—

We're all on our way to somewhere
Rarely stopping for a rest
Yet oblivious to why
We're even on this foolish quest

—

If we plan a life beholden
To some vision in our mind
We just limit our potential
To change what has been defined

We're conditioned to seek praise
For what we say, think, want and do
Which just sets us up for trouble
Bound to strive our whole lives through

——

If our lives are ever–changing
Is there anything that's true
Or will all we've come to cherish
Soon expire from our view?
Will we find some solid ground
On which to one day come to rest
Or a greater sense of meaning
Far beyond this futile quest?

My mind is off again today
Intent on running far away
To ruminate on what has been
Left floundering in past chagrin
And then it hastens miles ahead
Lamenting what will come instead
Of choosing to remain right here
Unbound by fate or yesteryear

———

Simply being in the moment
Cannot ever fill this need
To rush headlong through my time on earth
Besotted by the speed

———

If life just goes
As with the rose
Whose petals fade then fall
Ever armed to fight
Fate's ruthless might
Serves no intent at all

We will ever brandish swords
In life's battle for rewards
With no option to prevailing
Since we cannot venture failing

———

I never had the wherewithal
To linger in one place
Since escaping from my somber thoughts
Became a lifelong race

———

If we focus on the stars
Yet miss the ground beneath our feet
We'll live fettered by tomorrow
When each moment dawns replete

———

The duty of the brain
Should be to serve reality
Not propel us on a journey
Toward tomorrow's fantasy

I have finally reached the summit
Of this stunning mountaintop
Feeling utterly exhausted
And just desperate to stop
But the impulse to remain here
Captivated by the view
Cannot quench my inner fire
To keep blazing trails anew

—

O'er miles of this uncharted ground
I've come too far to turn around
But gazing at the trail ahead
I'm overcome by fear and dread
For though I've traveled night and day
In search of truth along the way
I've only just begun my quest
With trials unknown before I rest

Ever focused on the outcome
And achieving more each day
Has us racing past the beauty
Of the sights along the way

———

Our obsession with performance
Has us powerless to see
All the wonder right before us
Simply asking us to be

———

In our thirst for validation
We charge blindly toward the goal
Even though there isn't anything
Man truly can control

In knowing we are soon to die
Why do we still embrace the lie
Not face our fate courageously
All victims of mortality

———

What's the use in being
Just a pawn in life's cruel game
When no matter what I say or do
My fate is still the same?

I've been frantic to get somewhere
Yet still waiting to arrive
Though I push myself to triumph
And continually strive
To exceed all expectation
But forever seeking more
Since I haven't yet discovered
What I'm really searching for

———

Though I've lived a lot
And learned a lot
With latitude to grow
I will never find contentment
When my fate
I've yet to know

Madly focused on amassing
More possessions to debut
Leaves us little time to realize
What we're truly meant to do

———

A life that's fully planned
Is rife with pressure unabating
For it's shrouded from the wonder
Ever patiently awaiting

For those who race through every day
The time too quickly slips away
While those who live without a care
Can always find an hour to spare

———

The beauty of this spring day
Leaves me terribly downcast
For my time left here to savor it
Is waning much too fast

———

We thwart change by resisting time
Impelled to hold our breath
Though denying what's in constant flux
Just expedites our death

I've been racing ever madly
To outrun my heavy head
Making each and every moment
Action-packed to stem the dread
Never stopping for a respite
For I have no other choice
As I'm far too weak to vanquish
This demonic inner voice

———

For years I watched the world go by
Through windowpanes and wondered why
While others seemed to relish life
My head was filled with constant strife
And though my heart still deeply aches
I've now committed all it takes
To hurtle forward twice as fast
Reclaiming every moment passed

If life is one long journey
From our birth until our death
A vast road on which we travel
And explore with every breath
Then we must avoid becoming
Too enamored with the view
For we have such finite time
And so much more to see and do

———

We are ever streaming rivers
Just intent on rushing through
Certain life is much too busy
To enjoy the stunning view

Could it be
Another year
So quickly slipped away
For by every count
It seemed to last
No longer than a day
And if what's to come
Keeps hastening
At such a rapid pace
We'll soon come to find
Time has been crowned
Sole victor in this race

Most folks count down to their birthdays
I pretend they don't exist
For each new year brings me closer
To a fate I must resist

———

Until our minds and bodies
Find communion in one place
We'll remain forever searching
Running life's quixotic race

———

What's the point in laboring
To win this futile race
If we don't intend to leave the world
A vastly better place?

There's so much more
I need to do
So much I need to say
Yet such little time
To make my mark
Since death will have its way

———

All these years I raced in circles
To subdue this chronic pain
Certain unrelenting action
Would absolve my burdened brain
But no motion, plan, behavior
Or release of angst through rhyme
Could obscure the steady drumbeat
And incessant march of time

———

A mind that is essentially
Unsettled at its core
Cannot ever access peace
For it will always covet more

Regardless of what height I climb
To set myself above
And in spite of how I give myself
Intent to render love
And no matter how I help the sick
The feeble and the poor
And despite how I still stumble
When I long to run no more
And regardless of how often
My name flows off learned tongue
As the years go by this body
Will no longer feel as young
And no matter how I truly yearn
To take another breath
This life soon will be extinguished
By an uninvited death

Gray, gray
Go away
I need to keep
The years at bay

———

I can lose myself in nature
And seek solace penning rhyme
But no action ever quiets
This eternal march of time

———

I can practice meditation
And stay focused on each breath
But the stillness cannot silence
These persistent thoughts of death

There's never cause
For me to pause
And savor every breath
When just standing still
Won't ever fill
This looming void of death

———

In a world that's overflowing
With vast possibility
Certain never to be realized
With advancing destiny
We're left questioning life's purpose
Existentially encumbered
As the clock continues ticking
And our days grow ever numbered

When our days are filled
With superficial trivialities
We are veiled from both life's beauty
And its harsh realities
Chasing self-indulgent pleasures
And innumerable diversions
That inhibit us from taking
Vital soul-searching excursions

———

Though I'm petrified to ponder
This great mystery of death
With the vacuum ever waiting
Once we take our final breath
I will manifest the courage
And explore this certain fate
So perhaps I can look forward
To beyond my mortal state

I had spent my lifetime frantically
Pursuing the next thrill
With innumerable adventures
To avoid remaining still
Though I realized it was only
To escape an addled mind
Which raced faster than my body
Yet was desperate to unwind
So I focused on my breath
And learned to find contentment here
For perpetual commotion
Couldn't quell relentless fear

Every morn I trudge uphill
Though never reach the top
Which impels my battered body
To renounce the fight and stop
Yet I blindly hasten forward
To endure another day
Hopeful fate will heed my cries
And drive these mortal fears away

—

It really is quite comforting
To know death spares no living thing
Despite what they may say or do
The clock for them is ticking too

The current grabs my feeble frame
And plunges it downstream
I have nothing to grab onto
Nor a soul to hear me scream
As I hurtle ever blindly
Toward a truth I greatly fear
And the darkness calmly waiting
Absent all I hold so dear

———

He said "you'll be living
A great many years"
That did much to allay
Ever burgeoning fears
But from that time resolved
To live life with such ardor
I would never lament
For more time to try harder

If death becomes the cost
Of reaching immortality
I will gladly shed this form
That only serves to torment me

———

Only when this mortal body
Has been placed beneath the earth
Will I savor liberation
With a portal to rebirth

———

There can never be renewal
Without undergoing death
For transcendence only dawns
Once we have gasped our final breath

To reach our peak performance
Working systematically
We oft utilize a skill
Termed as rote "muscle memory"
In repeating basic tasks
Till they are altogether honed
And entail no conscious effort
So efficiently intoned
Yet to truly live a life
That rings with meaning and is true
We must fight the urge to mimic
And cleave novel pathways through

If death was right beside us
Ever whispering in our ears
It would surely make us question
Why we idled through the years

—

My heart just wants to soar
But my mind's demanding more
Ever frantic to know why
We endure though soon to die

What's the point in just subsisting
And why should we even try
With no refuge in persisting
Knowing everything must die

———

We spend every moment chasing
Something never really lost
In a race that proves in vain
And not remotely worth the cost
When in truth that which we're seeking
Waits suspended deep inside
Needing earnest introspection
To become our faithful guide

———

Endless action masks unhappiness
So when we cease our racing
We'll be left to contemplate
The void exposed bereft all chasing

As long as we're fixated
On tomorrow chasing dreams
Brainwashed by the core belief
There's more to life than what it seems
We'll neglect the chance to heed
Our soul's most elemental cry
Or develop strength to trust
That on ourselves we can rely

———

When I'm lying on my deathbed
And reflecting on past days
Will the heartache that torments me now
Still trigger such malaise?

If we hasten down life's pathway
Rarely gazing side to side
Wholly focused on the future
And maintaining constant stride
We'll not find the time to access
Our authentic voice within
And deny ourselves the gift
Of reaping all that could have been

We spend lifetimes racing rabidly
On foot, rails, boats or planes
Always on our way to somewhere
In the search for fresh domains
Yet we cannot find through motion
What lies dormant in our soul
And involves no destination
Just awareness absent goal

If death affords acquittal
From reality we know
To commence a new adventure
Granting everlasting flow
Then it surely shouldn't garner
Such anxiety and dread
But allow us to meet fate
With curiosity instead

As we pass our final hours
With a lifetime in rewind
What will prove the brightest moments
Left imprinted on our mind?
Which travails will be remembered
For the lessons they inspired
What accomplishments exalted
For the wisdom that transpired?
Who'll have been those loyal comrades
Standing proudly by our side
Through the struggles of existence
Always willing to provide?
And if only we revealed these truths
Before our final breath
We could focus on what mattered most
Instead of fearing death

HYPOCRISY AND DUALITY

I just so blatantly saw others' and my own duplicity—both intolerant of myself for being who I was but also others for being who they were as well.

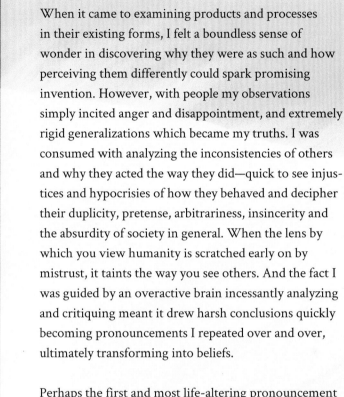

When it came to examining products and processes in their existing forms, I felt a boundless sense of wonder in discovering why they were as such and how perceiving them differently could spark promising invention. However, with people my observations simply incited anger and disappointment, and extremely rigid generalizations which became my truths. I was consumed with analyzing the inconsistencies of others and why they acted the way they did—quick to see injustices and hypocrisies of how they behaved and decipher their duplicity, pretense, arbitrariness, insincerity and the absurdity of society in general. When the lens by which you view humanity is scratched early on by mistrust, it taints the way you see others. And the fact I was guided by an overactive brain incessantly analyzing and critiquing meant it drew harsh conclusions quickly becoming pronouncements I repeated over and over, ultimately transforming into beliefs.

Perhaps the first and most life-altering pronouncement came in the way I viewed people. Because once I looked at others as evil, that "*truism*" traveled the path from mistrust to profound disappointment, disillusionment and then finally to intense derision and cynicism toward all humanity. Yet despite knowing this overly-judgmental mindset would never be embraced by society, I couldn't seem to control my reactions. I just so blatantly saw others' and my own duplicity—both intolerant of myself for being who I was but also others for being who they were as well.

First and foremost, I couldn't accept the fact that no one *"understood the ephemeral nature of existence,"* squandering time like a basic commodity. Others were laughing, dancing and flitting around without a care in the world when their lives were evaporating right before their very eyes. In fact, such wanton careless-ness made no sense to me at all. They would literally soon be dust—and this was how they were choosing to spend their remaining moments? Doing absolutely nothing of worth or meaning leading them to legacy or immortality? Why didn't they get it? How could they act as if they didn't have a care in the world (care-free) when I was so miserable (care-full) and hearing the call of mortality each and every day? In fact, I was all but shouting plain truths at the top of my lungs while the rest of the world gawked dumbfounded, unable to process my message. I didn't want to seem like a know-it-all, but why weren't they reacting to blatant reality? This just reinforced how I would never fit in, left wondering why what seemed so obvious wasn't shared by anyone else. And as disgusted and critical as I was of them, I was actually most enraged with myself for the inability to be like them, left succumbing to a fate I was helpless to alter. I so desperately wanted to live free enough to dance and sing with complete abandon and behave as if tomorrow didn't matter, but unfortunately tomorrow was all I ever thought and worried about. Tomorrow was just a time bomb ticking away to my final breath.

I eventually surmised that the reason others could live so freely had to be some combination of: 1) they didn't see the truth, 2) they didn't believe the truth, 3) they didn't understand the truth, or 4) they didn't care life was passing them by, yet were doing nothing to make the most of it. However, I did feel a bit superior knowing the joke was ultimately on them. No matter how ardently they played, joked, laughed and masked the truth, they would soon be extinguished with absolutely nothing to show for their brief time here. They would lose in their idiotic game to thwart death. Knowing the reality of existence made me feel somewhat relieved, but still left me bewildered why I was the only one who had received the outline for the final and was preparing for the test.

I also continually questioned senseless realities of the human condition such as the fallibility of our mortal bodies. As miraculous as these bodies were in totality, how could they be so fundamentally barbaric, repulsively animalistic, and disappointingly deficient when they should be impervious and transcend terminal form? For starters, I couldn't believe how revolting the human body smelled. So horrible, in fact, there were entire industries built around masking those smells—from mouthwashes and toothpastes to gums, soaps, shampoos, body-washes, lotions and deodorants, to perfumes, air fresheners, bathroom sprays, candles, potpourris and car deodorizers to boot. Why would we be housed in a body smelling so appallingly bad? And if that wasn't enough, the sounds emanating from our bodies were simply hideous and shame-inducing— snoring, snorting, burping, farting, slurping, chewing and stomach gurgling seemed so beneath our mind's capabilities and who we aspired to be spiritually and intellectually.

I was further appalled at the burgeoning business segments built around hair removal (even permanently with laser machines), as their sole mission was to make us less animal-like by removing the hair covering our beastly bodies. I could never reconcile these two extremes—the mind and soul so highly evolved and seemingly immortal in their expansiveness, pitted directly against a barbaric, ephemeral, aging, decaying, carnal vessel ultimately betraying us by perishing and turning to dust. Being imprisoned in this weak, fleshy, mortal body devastated and left me questioning the inanity of existence.

My soul was yearning to soar freely with no limits, and yet the body in which it resided was deteriorating with each passing moment. In fact, it was utterly apocalyptic to witness the injustice of multitudes of elderly in the throes of massive atrophy, left abandoned in establishments created solely for the purpose of stashing them somewhere until their demise. My grandmother had eventually expired in one of those institutions and the smell alone was absolutely revolting—one of excrement, disease, deterioration and decay. I couldn't

fathom undergoing that same process—determined to
have my body remain a flawless, impenetrable specimen
never smelling, faltering or crumbling. Strangely, I had
somehow always believed myself to be beyond mere
mortal existence and the chosen one to attain immortality. After all, I had spent an entire lifetime controlling
all inputs entering my temple and keeping it free of
medicines, alcohol, drugs and food toxins by taking
exceptional care, while also exercising without fail seven
days a week. So I deserved more than anyone to triumph
over destiny. And yet, despite my laborious efforts, I still
found myself suffering the same ailments, aches, pains,
exhaustion and perpetual aging as everyone else.

Even young people, I observed, were falling victim to
maladies they were powerless to repel, with scores of
children's hospitals overrun with youth suffering cancers
and diseases ravaging their bodies leaving them entirely
defenseless. Our culture obsessively took vitamins and
supplements, ate costly organic food, visited doctors
regularly for physicals and exercised incessantly, yet we
were powerless against the march of time and havoc it
wreaked on our bodies. If the human form had been
created to protect us against the ills and poisons of
the merciless world, why was it virtually defenseless
to forestall our impending fate and literally decaying
from birth? That just couldn't be the "*plan*"—leaving
me certain I must manage these forces and change this
destined outcome, though at a complete loss on how
to effectively do so.

In the end, I also saw my own duality, baffled how
I could give such a phony impression to the outside
world yet feel so entirely different inside; behave
as if I didn't have a single care when in reality was
terrified and riddled with despair; or feel insecure and
overwhelmed one day but ready to conquer the world
the next. And yet, my flawless demeanor ensured no
one would see the anguish I was masking. It just didn't
make sense I could be two so totally opposite sides of
the same coin, and completely shield all fallibility from
others to conceal my true essence. And ultimately,
I was left with the clear contention I would never
understand or have ability to control my emotions,
my fate, the passage of time, or human nature and its
ever-changing wiles...

It just didn't make sense I could be two so totally opposite sides of the same coin, and completely shield all fallibility from others to conceal my true essence.

Some days I feel such joy
I should be tethered to a chair
Or I'd surely rise above the clouds
And lose myself up there
Yet on others feel so low
I could be swallowed by the ground
Suffocated by the sadness
With no impulse to be found

—

If when sorrows come we hang our heads
And speculate "why me"
We must do the same with joys
As they're indeed just as likely
Or we'll form the wrong impression
We're predestined to despair
When in truth life's such a blessing
And our mindset that's unfair

The urge to know ourselves
Becomes the root of all desire
Though our fear of digging in
Then disallows it to transpire

———

The duplicity of who we are
Is tough to reconcile
When our true selves never surface
From a lifetime in denial

———

Who the ego thinks we are
Provokes a lifetime full of pain
For it's merely an invention
To entrap us in the brain

It's a challenge to stay healthy
In a culture that is ill
And cannot be simply cured
With a prescription for a pill

————

Since beliefs become reality
Then what if they are wrong
And create the misconception
We will never quite belong
Thereby filling us with distrust
Isolated and depressed
With our yearning for connection
Left forever unexpressed

————

We must strive for concrete action
In a world that has no meaning
For inertia will prevail
Without persistent intervening

It's a shame
We only honor
Those outstanding qualities
Of our loved ones
Once they pass away
Expressed as memories

———

Wisdom comes with age some say
But I believe naiveté
Increases with each passing year
And now what I most deeply fear
Is that the more I come to know
The more confused this mind will grow
And lost will be the chance to see
The world with any clarity

———

It takes a person dying
To remember what was best
And appreciate their essence
Disregarding all the rest

We must always look for reasons
To explain how someone acts
Though we tend to implicate them
Before knowing all the facts

———

Who's to judge who has true freedom
Or who spends their lives enslaved
Who's to judge who is a victim
Or who's utterly depraved
For we never will exist
Within another's heart and brain
And can't claim to know their story
Or the context for their pain

———

Might there be a silver lining
To a lifetime of conforming
Ever shielded from the pressure
Of perpetually performing?

If only we were thinner
Bolder, wittier and bright
Then our lives would swell with meaning
And we'd find contentment, right?
But alas, that's not the case
For once we aired those qualities
We'd just set our sights on new ones
Bound to never feel at ease

—

Though I'm certain formal process
Never furthers innovation
It may prove a worthy tool
In sparking personal salvation
Granting necessary framework
To inspire self-reflection
Then becoming so innate
We're free to chart our own direction

My gaze is steady
Head held high
Inside I'm shaking
Scared and shy
I walk with purpose
Straight and tall
Inside I'm curled up
In a ball
I smile, joke, giggle
Flirt and tease
Inside I'm screaming,
"Help me, please!"

———

I lived behind a pretense
And the world could never see
All the raging inner turmoil
Which served quite effectively

Are we satisfied existing
As the characters we play
Or more desperate to broadcast
Our most honest truths each day?

———

No one sees our essence
For we take such care to hide
Our amazing superpowers
And parade the phony side

———

Are we destined to perform
As actors shrouded in disguise
Or aspiring to utter
Our most heartfelt inner cries?

What happens in the world
Is viewed through our specific lens
Which means how we choose to act
Most undeniably depends
On particular experience
Defining what we see
And informing our perceptions
Rising from that history

—

What if the truth was different
Than our minds let us believe
And the stories we repeated
Only serving to deceive
Us from accessing the answers
That would set our spirits free
From a lifetime spent denying
Who we're truly meant to be

No one has an inkling
Of just who we are inside
When the only part we brandish
Is the superficial side

———

Stop pretending that you know me
From the markings on my shell
Which give no sign I am frantic
To escape this inner hell

———

Don't observe how I'm attired
And presume to read my soul
What's revealed upon the surface
Has scant likeness to the whole

We search for truth
In others' eyes
When in our own
Gleam countless lies

———

We lie, lust, cheat
Judge, steal then pray
Convinced our sins
Will wash away

———

Our egos have us forging homes
Baronial in size
Yet with little warmth within
Since they've been built for others' eyes

I am so wise
In others' eyes
But in my own a fool
Advice I give
I fail to live
And let emotion rule

————

I can write, teach and profess
The simple truths I need to know
And yet when it comes to living them
I've countless miles to go

————

My laughter sounds quite joyous
But it's masking how I feel
For I'm loathe to show my true self
Knowing what it would reveal

Through prayer we aim to change
The way the universe is working
By imploring God to offer
What our souls are slyly shirking
For one cannot bend the rules
Of what has been or what will be
And we must accept our fate
To access true autonomy

———

Religion is a way
Of making sense of our despair
By affording us the promise
That salvation waits out there

———

While knowledge is pure truth
Our learned perception's just a way
Of converting to illusion
How we view the world each day

I'm scared to live life
Yet more frightened to die
I'm scared to inquire
Yet intent to know why
I'm scared to resound
Yet can't live without song
I'm scared to speak up
Yet compelled to right wrong
I'm scared to feel joy
Yet deplore constant pain
I'm scared to stand out
Yet disgusted by plain
I'm scared to feel hope
Yet detest constant dread
I'm scared to take charge
Yet despise being led
I'm scared to need help
Yet can't function this way
I'm scared for my fate
Yet must conquer today

We've conceived complex contraptions
To protect our fragile form
From scarves, heaters and wool mittens
So in winter we'll keep warm
To umbrellas and galoshes
So we'll not be touched by rain
And elixirs for each ailment
To dull all effects of pain
Costly wrinkle creams and face lifts
Mask the dreaded signs of age
As mass weapons of destruction
Foster skirmishes to wage
So complex and so consuming
Today's struggle to survive
There's no time left for rejoicing
In the fact that we're alive

We point the blame at others
Rarely gazing deep inside
For it's simpler to condemn
Than our hypocrisy confide

———

We're quick to pause
At others' flaws
Yet rarely see our own
For whenever we
Gaze outwardly
Our souls remain unknown

———

We bully others
And condemn
Ignore ourselves
Intent on them
Afraid to look
Inside our hearts
Where victimizing
Always starts

Some days I feel quite powerful
Yet others frail and meek
Either shouting from the rooftops
Or afraid to even speak

——

Some days I act so big and strong
And others weak and small
Either moving mighty mountains
Or afraid to move at all

Some days I'm such an optimist
And others very low
Either planning my next escapade
Or drowned in utter woe

———

Some days I'm flush in anguish
With no reason to survive
Others leaping over mountaintops
Just thrilled to be alive

I breathe darkness
I shine light
I fall victim
I wage fight
I seek joy
I fuel despair
I act blind
I stay aware
I give comfort
I wreak pain
I grant praise
I show disdain
I shout loudly
I bow meek
I stand strong
I play weak
I raise honor
I bear shame
I seem different
I feel same

continues »

I cry anguish
I find hope
I am drowning
I can cope
I keep clinging
I soar free
I am phony
I am me

The sun is shining
Yet I think rain
My body's healthy
Yet I feel pain
The day shows promise
Yet I sense doom
The future's bright
Yet I see gloom
The praise is flowing
Yet I hear doubt
My cup is full
Yet I fear drought
My head is pounding
Please send relief
I cannot bear
This constant grief

Why are most content to squander
Their brief moments here on earth
Wholly rapt in idle wantonness
Frivolity and mirth?

—

I am struggling
Ever struggling
To find meaning here on earth
Asking why
All those around me
Are awash in endless mirth

—

What if death was celebrated
With our birth a time to grieve
For birth meant a life imprisoned
And demise a nice reprieve

How can I make them happy
When I hold such grief inside
How can they build deep friendships
When my tendency's to hide?
How can they trust in others
When I've always felt betrayed
How can they find their voices
When I've lived my life afraid?
How they feel expectant
When I'm clearly so unsure
How can they stick their necks out
When I'm weak and insecure?
How can they mirror wholeness
When I'm largely incomplete
How can they hasten forward
When I'm toppled by defeat?
How can they find their passions
When I've plainly lost my way
How can I give them courage
When I'm paralyzed today?

Within the frames
In our front hall
Are smiling faces
Special places
Featured on the wall
And those who pause
On their way through
To casually view
Have little cause
To find portrayed
A story other
Or face another
Than appears displayed
Yet dressed in frames
Upon the wall
Live countless lies
For past those eyes
No smiles exist at all

There is no such thing
As peace of mind
For minds are not at peace
And it's only
Absent mind
That we will ever find release

———

Every glowing word you stated
Left me utterly forsaken
Since your sweet talk wasn't matched
With heartfelt actions ever taken

———

Trying to act grandiose
Or trying to act small
Are really just two masks we wear
And not unlike at all
As both roles employ the ego
And the struggle to be seen
Ever moved by expectations
To define what life should mean

I'm a warrior
With no courage left to fight
I'm a perfectionist
With no skill left to be right
I'm a dreamer
With no passion left to hope
I'm an adult
With no wisdom left to cope
I'm an player
With no friends left to care
I'm a poet
With no words left to share
I'm a mother
With no comfort left to give
I am drowning
With no will left to live

How man can live so close to death
Suspended by a single breath
Yet fill his days with hope instead
Of fearing what may lie ahead
Is truly a courageous thing
And certainly inspiring

———

The more I dream,
Hope, want and try
The more life tends
To go awry
And times at which
I hardly care
Find fortune
Springs up everywhere!

Why do those who have so little
Offer gratitude galore
Whereas others who have everything
Attempt to covet more?

———

He needs more
And I want less
We're really just
The same I guess
Since he's not wrong
And I'm not right
But simply how
We wage our fight

———

Some crave solace
Some want speed
With shared intent
Yet novel need

To listen and to hear
Although similar appear
Are quite different indeed
Even though both use the ear

———

How dare you say "I love you"
Without knowing me at all
Having never cared to infiltrate
This shrouded inner wall

———

Am I the courage
Others see
Or coward crouched
Inside of me?

———

Am I the vision
Others see
Or grief that
Nearly buries me?

Goals are simple to state
Yet not easy to do
Which is why we speak more
Than just following through

———

My soul is now ascending
Yet my mind is still contending
What the future has in store
Since it cannot help me soar

———

I am torn between my need
To make a difference every day
And spend all my time in nature
With no outcome to display

If my prayers
Are truly answered
Then what will I ever do?
For my mind
Will go on craving
Further fancies to pursue!

———

We can pilfer someone's honor
And not label it a crime
For infractions of indignity
Will never serve jail time
Yet are surely as deceptive
As pickpockets on the street
Though impossible to sentence
When their damage stays discreet

———

Calling someone unattractive
Doesn't make you more appealing
Just shows callous disregard
For how those words leave others feeling

Though some go through life appearing
So audacious and assured
Doesn't mean they're not afflicted
By the hardships they've endured

———

Though we're sheltered for nine months
Inside a well-protected womb
Doesn't mean our host will be
The doting mother we'd assume
For caregiving isn't always
Biological in nature
And sustaining someone else
Needs no established nomenclature

———

All my words are cloaked in darkness
Yet my playthings bathed in light
For within this fluid being
Grief resides while hope burns bright

True talent isn't born
From simply sharpening a skill
But is gifted from within
And predetermined to fulfill

———

I kindly ask
You shed the mask
Before you step inside
So I can see
You honestly
With nothing left to hide

———

They say ignorance is bliss
But clearly ignorance is pain
For when blinded from the truth
Our whole existence is in vain

Thank goodness we don't know
What will befall us in advance
So we're able to live peacefully
And leave all else to chance

———

Though there's comfort in complacency
And moving with the herd
Those who truly strive for greatness
Find that utterly absurd

———

I've always found it crazy
That my peers appeared so lazy
With no wherewithal to flee
Lives of mediocrity

It's much simpler granting empathy
To victims we don't know
Than to those who've truly wronged us
Which unleashes our ego

———

Why do some defend so doggedly
The rights of those unseen
Yet denounce their blood relations
With such ardor to demean?

———

We can only offer others
What exists within to give
And must purify the soul
So love remains within the sieve

———

When ideas are "set in stone"
Our need for answers leads the way
When perception is organic
With new insights every day

The same set of circumstances
Can be viewed in different ways
Which determine whether we rejoice
Or wallow in malaise

———

Any situation
Can be heaven or pure hell
Simply based on our perceptions
And the stories our minds tell

———

There's no person who can steal our heart
And lock it in a cell
Only misinformed beliefs
Which serve to sentence us in hell

To navigate each day
Existing utterly unseen
Offers both a gift and curse
Depending what it comes to mean
For although most wouldn't choose
To live eternally alone
When beholden to no other
Every action is their own

———

Today's learning begs clear answers
Graded either wrong or right
Education in two boxes
One marked black, the other white
When there can't be rote solutions
To the issues of today
And it's only through invention
We'll devise a better way

When learning is reduced
To spewing notes back on a test
Schooling centers on performance
Not an ardent knowledge quest
With facts idling in the head
Instead of quickening the heart
Left bereft of deeper wisdom
Though our grades imply we're smart

———

We spend every moment striving
To feel utterly secure
In a universe whose essence
Is elusive and unsure

———

Fulfillment isn't found
By how much money's in the bank
Or the status amply crowned
From reaching elevated rank
But in probing who we are
Devoid a superficial role
Free to access our North Star
And truly gratify our soul

VOLUME EIGHT

CURIOSITY

I was born rabidly curious, eager to decipher life's most puzzling mysteries and understand the incongruities of the world in which I lived.

I was born rabidly curious, eager to decipher life's most puzzling mysteries and understand the incongruities of the world in which I lived. I forever asked *"why"* with the insatiable desire to make sense of everything occurring around me and determine why it was happening. In fact, I would often sit bolt upright in the middle of the night with an inquiry burning such a hole in my brain I had no choice but to get up and write it down in order to fall back to sleep. I pondered everything from the doom and gloom of *"why do we die and what happens when we die?"* to other more basic enigmas such as, *"what determines the patterning on butterfly wings and number of spots on a ladybug?" "how can every snowflake look different?"* and *"what is the value of ticks?"* And probably the question I contemplated most as a child was: *"how can tears represent both happiness and sadness, yet not look any different when someone is crying them?"*

I was ever perplexed none of my peers seemed to ponder life's absurdities, never asking probing questions or seeking to understand why things were the way they were. They viewed my ruminations as inconsequential and weird, regarding me disdainfully if I ever disclosed one in their company. I therefore had no choice but to conceal my incessant quest for answers from the world. It didn't stop the fact that I still fervently sought explanations, but I knew from early on I was alone in my avid pursuit of knowledge.

Absorbing information as rapidly as possible became
an obsession as I matured. I felt perpetual panic there
was so much material to read, watch and consume that
I would miss out on that one insight forever impacting
my thinking and changing my life. It was essentially
the same Fear of Missing Out and insatiable *"desire for
more"* ever tormenting me. And yet, I truly delighted in
discovering a revelatory nugget of insight enabling me
to think about or view the world differently. There was
nothing sweeter than understanding a topic thoroughly
enough to engage in critical analysis and derive inventive
conclusions across multiple disciplines. Drawing novel,
unconventional observations from seemingly ordinary,
unremarkable data truly intoxicated me.

I was utterly captivated by words and delighted in
dissecting their meaning, especially compound words
where both halves came together to forge richer
definitions. I contemplated those ending in *"full (ful)"*
and *"less,"* the dichotomy of fear-ful (full of fear) versus
fear-less (not having fear), help-ful versus help-less
and harm-ful versus harm-less. But consequently,
I never understood the meanings of mind-ful and
mind-less. Supposedly our goal in life was to become
more mind-full (mindful), and yet my personal goal
was clearly to become more mind-less. After all, the fact
that my mind was so full was what agonized me each
day! I understood the word had come to mean being
more *"aware,"* but for me more aware meant leaving
my mind and living more in my heart. So I personally

strived to become mind-less and heart-full, thereby perplexed why we used the word mindful. I actually wrote a verse about this paradox as it frustrated me to such an extent! And lastly, I questioned why individuals were called *self-ish* rather than *self-ful,* leaving me unable to comprehend such incongruities of the English language that made absolutely no sense!

I especially relished leaving the world of people, expectations and performance and becoming a seeker rife with curiosity. In the realm of discovery, I was never one bit cynical but brimming with awe, wonder and boundless possibility—a sponge passionately craving further wisdom and desperate to make sense of existence by refining incongruities into their most basic form. Just as I simplified my innermost feelings into plain words, I needed to do the same with ideas and arguments, ruthlessly trying to explain findings in easily digestible terms. It was essential to wholly comprehend the very derivation of ideas in order to effectively process them and draw meaningful conclusions.

Given I required adequate deliberation time to interpret data for thorough understanding, I could never quickly respond to questions with knee-jerk answers. In fact, I called myself a *"distiller"* in requiring input to gently wash over and settle into my being with time and space to ponder before deriving a wholly informed and honest assessment. I thus often asked others to slowly restate their comments so I could meaningfully process

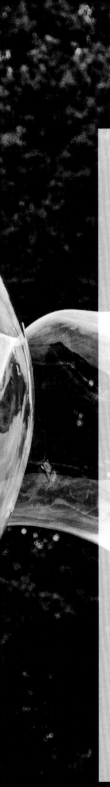

them, the one always raising her hand in meetings and querying, *"I'm sorry but I don't get it"* or *"I get what you're saying but it doesn't make sense to me."*

This simplistic mentality wasn't generally perceived kindly, garnering disgusted head shakes and eye rolls from my peers (although some occasionally admitted they were also confused yet ashamed to admit their ignorance). And although unsettling when others showed annoyance with my extended period of deliberation, I was surprisingly never remorseful over trying to process ideas and needing time to do so. My desire to absorb information fully so I could develop insight and effectively draw conclusions was just too great to feign understanding. In this and only this instance, I didn't even care what others thought of me, because my drive to fully comprehend concepts in order to further learning and creation was so intense!

I found the magic of discovery in spaces between deep, organic observation and formal research, for there was an intoxicating and profound magic in understanding a topic so fully I could close my eyes and pause, allowing revelations to bubble up out of the hush of white space. I was certain answers to even the world's most pressing dilemmas were always patiently waiting, but shrouded in layers of discovery requiring excavation for exposure. That involved research then reflection—taking time and diligence to unearth all the clues, deliberately process data so dots

"Discovery is seeing what everyone has seen and thinking what no one has thought."

DR. ALBERT SZENT-GYORGYI

could connect innately, and then organically enable epiphanies to shine through. It was actually a sacred ritual in intentionally collecting every precious insight and allowing them to naturally synthesize to reveal innovative solutions. Disparate insights, research and instinct crystallizing within to emerge in a *"eureka moment"* was so profoundly divine that I called it *"the angels singing."* For it was truly as if every star in the universe had aligned in such manner that the heavens opened to give birth to a stunning revelation.

I actually loved seeing the world differently and thinking about thinking in a revelatory manner. In fact, my favorite quote came from Dr. Albert Szent-Gyorgyi who stated, *"Discovery is seeing what everyone has seen and thinking what no one has thought."* I was exhilarated by the quest to take what seemed ordinary and perceive it in an entirely revolutionary manner to make it extraordinary, certain this mindset was the essence of innovation, experiencing life and the method by which humanity and society advanced.

I summed up my mindset toward innovation as follows: *"Being an innovator means seeing the world in all its possibility with potential to augment any aspect. It is a mindset of wholly opening oneself up to wonder—ever curious and questioning the why behind what currently exists and seeing it rife with optimism and potential to be different. It means distilling a product, service or process down to the very essence of how it functions and honestly assessing whether its outcome is profoundly captivating or intensely impactful. And if the experience is flawed in any sense, envisioning how it can be reinvented to become richer and more meaningful. It is the belief nothing needs to be as it is—it can become whatever we imagine it to be."*

I truly reveled in being a knowledge seeker despite the fact others didn't seem to possess the same voracious appetite I had to further learning. My peers had no interest in rabidly pondering and critiquing the way people, processes and products functioned, or engaging in intense research believing it much too laborious. Yet I was thoroughly enraptured by the discovery process, as the acquisition of knowledge was truly wonder-filled, my preferred pastime, and never viewed as work at all. And I knew it separated me from others not enjoying or wishing to engage in the quest for truth. In fact, the more complex a challenge or problem, the more I enjoyed deciphering the solution. Being a *"forger of white space"* and finding opportunity wherever my curiosity took me was as close to nirvana as I could get, armed with supreme power to tap into the boundless realm of imagination and make the impossible absolute reality.

POSSIBILITY

My ultimate power came in striving to live my life authentically in doing what I believed was right, and treating others with compassion.

I had spent an entire lifetime believing I was at the whim of forces out of my control—namely mortality, relationships, circumstances and my choices. And I was drowning in futility over trying so desperately to control the uncontrollable, but no closer to doing so than I had ever been. However, I finally came to see that the only aspects of existence I could actually control were the attitude with which I greeted each day, the specific actions I took to live a meaningful life, and the manner by which I responded to and treated those around me. My ultimate power came in striving to live my life authentically in doing what I believed was right, and treating others with compassion. I then needed to accept the ramifications, good or bad, from that sincere behavior, because I wasn't going to change others through bitterness and wishing they were different, yet totally poison myself with hostility, living life eternally miserable. I already had a predisposition to starting each day despondent, and was perpetuating that mindset with negativity and blame regarding my circumstances. It was therefore imperative to take ownership of my perceptions, my attitude, and my behavior. Additionally, I needed to make certain my inner circle exuded only positive energy lifting me up to live wholly in my heart.

Instead of waking up every morning certain *"life wasn't fair," "why was this happening to me?"* and *"I can't take this anymore"* as if powerless with nothing in my control, I started answering those statements with: *"You do have control and a choice Melissa. If you are so miserable*

then just end your life, because that is entirely your decision." After all, I could choose the actions, mindset and attitude with which I greeted each day. This meant I could either succumb to suffocating despair, or stop *"hoping"* circumstances would inevitably improve and fight to claw my way out of darkness. Although finding that light was horribly challenging most days and virtually impossible others, the choice to embrace life and endeavor to do so was entirely my own.

Thankfully, I now recognized I wasn't choosing to end my life and had never chosen to do so. And although acting like a weak, spineless victim and continually complaining about my circumstances, I was actually taking positive action each day in choosing to live rather than die. This meant I must somehow feel a sense of hope for the future! Yet despite that small spark of possibility, I was still wallowing in negativity, never turning despair into purpose-driven action and left exhausted and victimized, battered by the current with seemingly no way back to shore.

This attitude change from a helpless victim to one taking responsibility for her life choices alleviated that deep sense of hopelessness in bringing order to chaos. This major awakening lesson became: we can choose life and the attitude with which we greet each day. Or said differently, we can continue to drown in despair, or take concrete action and channel our pain into positive creation and connection. I was so convinced I needed to formalize this behavior change in moving forward, I wrote a pledge making it official:

"I, Melissa Bernstein, have a choice to make each day. I can either wallow in misery, imprisoned in my head ranting, raving and blaming others for my state, or choose to greet the world with positivity and desire to live life fully. Doing so doesn't necessarily mean I will succeed, but will commit myself to being a joy and light seeker all remaining moments of my life. That means I will not allow dark days to convince me there are no light ones ahead—rather see them as part of life knowing sunlight is always waiting above the clouds. Choosing life also means I will offer self-kindness and compassion, no longer inflicting harm in criticizing, berating, starving, exhausting, second-guessing and tormenting myself. Given I will respect my entire being, I will ask others do the same, clearly expressing my feelings and no longer allowing them to offend, hurt, overuse or maltreat me. I am choosing life and making a commitment to living honestly and gratefully each day here-forth."

At the end of the day it was actually all about control, yet not a lack of control as I had always believed. In fact, I held ultimate control over life with my mindset, my choices, and the power to write my own life story. And I could continue operating misguided by the sense each day was filled with despair, or believe differently and more optimistically that life had the potential to be joyous and fulfilling. It was entirely up to me.

*We can continue
to drown in despair,
or take concrete action
and channel our pain
into positive creation
and connection.*

It's quite easy to convince ourselves
The world is rife with doom
Spending decades disillusioned
And submerged in utter gloom
Till we realize nothing good
Can come from negativity
And our lives will be much sweeter
Living optimistically

We can choose to see the world
Awash in joy or steeped in gloom
For a wasteland can transform
Into a garden flush with bloom
If we open up our eyes
And simply revel in each day
Finding promise reigns supreme
With blue skies waiting past the gray

———

There's a predetermined number
Of times every heart will beat
Yet that knowledge mustn't cause
Us to surrender to defeat
Rather spur us to make meaning
In the span of finite years
And live every waking moment
Moved by joys instead of fears

If every bit of doom, dread, fear
And abject misery
Could evaporate into thin air
Allowing us to be
Just wholeheartedly our truest selves
With nothing in the way
Then we'd never squander precious time
Bemoaning life each day

Everything derives from fear
But can dissolve with love
Just as sunlight will break through
Storm clouds which threaten from above

———

It may take a tragic ending
To relinquish chapters past
And embark on new adventures
With potential truly vast

———

Though we can't void former misdeeds
We can alter judgments cast
And move forward with intention
To surmount our blemished past

Why do we keep complaining
Yet forever stay the same
Not use every breath remaining
To spark others with our flame?

———

Our duration here on earth
Is much too brief for misery
And we make every effort
To live optimistically

———

If you do the work you cherish
You will cherish what you do
And impart that boundless joy
To others seeking all that's true

Though it's easy to view others
As deceitful and unkind
When so often their behaviors
Are unconscionably blind
We must manifest compassion
Looking past that which seems cruel
With the faith those misdemeanors
Are exceptions not the rule

I now see a light
At the end of the path
I now grasp the why
For this internal wrath
I now read the signs
The crusade's worth the pain
I now have belief
Judging all's not in vain
I now trust I hold
Endless power to shape
I now clutch a key
And the chance to escape
I now feel I burst
With true wisdom to share
I now think I've learned
To wrest joy from despair
I now sense I'm filled
With creation to give
I now know I've found
Hope and reason to live

We must find the strength to navigate
Life's most distressing blows
Knowing joys are always waiting
In the shadow of their woes

—

Despite what evil's lurking
We must hasten toward the light
Where our darkest hours will soon give way
To moments shining bright

I have little time for those
Who choose to wallow in despair
Fearful, anxious and complaining
Certain life has been unfair
When our moments here on earth
Are much too brief to waste away
And we must remain intentional
To find hope every day

Although hope may live tomorrow
We can access it today
With the fortitude to navigate
Whatever comes our way

———

It's much easier to wallow
In despair than in delight
For the signs that life is bleaker
Are more prevalent than bright
And must authorize awareness
To illuminate the way
Letting every moment ground us
In the promise of today

How I wish I could convince you
That the future will be bright
Though you'd surely not believe me
When you cannot access light
But I promise if you reach out
To let those who love you in
You'll transcend the isolation
And redemption will begin

The best adjusted folks
Are those who never fitted in
For they needed to forge courage
From the wellspring deep within

———

There comes a point in life
When we've a vital choice to make
For our future is dependent
On which avenue we take
Either traveling the channel
Of resistance and repression
Or advancing toward the soul
Intent on hearing its confession

Shine the light you wish to see
Spread the joy you yearn to feel
Speak the truth you long to hear
Share the love you crave to heal
Soar beyond your separate self
Seeking oneness with all life
For connection is the portal
To transcend our inner strife

There is nothing more fulfilling
Than to face our destiny
With a plenitude of courage
And vast curiosity

———

It's not what we think that changes us
But how we think instead
For it governs if we live each day
In harmony or dread

———

We can focus on what's wrong in life
Or focus on what's right
But whatever we most focus on
Will aptly wield its might

What does it mean
To abandon the past
And surrender control
Knowing fate's die is cast
To renounce needless thought
And relinquish all fear
Guided purely by heart
Now awake to what's here

——

Surrender means we choose
To finally put away our swords
And stop fighting for success
With its material rewards

——

If all the fears
That filled my head
Were pleasant memories instead
I'd live each day
In total bliss
Content to only reminisce

We cannot resist time's passage
For it's destined to advance
So let's treasure every moment
And let fate control the dance

———

Journey into the unknown
Without a compass or trail guide
Flush with sheer exhilaration
And profoundly terrified

I moved from feeling
Deeply flawed
Imprisoned in my head
To now living life
Profoundly awed
Awash in joy instead

———

Though for years I wholly lost myself
In doom, despair and fear
I now live each day contented
And so grateful to be here

———

I have grieved for many years
Cried an ocean full of tears
Ever victimized by death
Yet defying with each breath

I have indeed
Confirmed the truth
Sheer wisdom doesn't
Come with youth
Nor with a mere
Advance in age
Can one profess
To be a sage
For wisdom is
Reserved for those
Who struggle through
Life's abject woes
And revel in
Profound insight
To help the rest
Emit their light

There's no need to gaze beyond
That which is simply in our view
When suspended in these confines
Lingers everything that's true

—

In an age where chasing dreams
Allows no time for rest it seems
And often led astray for miles
Enticed by cunning and its wiles
How nice it is some still remain
Immune to malice and disdain
Pursuing quite deliberately
A lifetime of integrity

Aversion
To not knowing
Keeps us curious
And growing

———

The same mind that holds us captive
Trapped in ego, doubts and fears
Also sparks the search for wisdom
In exploring new frontiers

———

We can't change what is
But can transform what will be
With the power to move forward
Thinking optimistically

———

Stop bemoaning what is destined
And embrace what you can do
There's still time to make a difference
Living every day anew

Don't succumb to life's frustrations
And find courage to push through
Since each day is filled with moments
To affect the world anew

———

If we revel in life's promise
Seeking presence every day
We'll entrust ourselves to making
Every breath be all it may

Life is filled
With lows and highs
As raging storms
Birth clear blue skies

———

We must expect
Both highs and lows
For only clouds
Conceive rainbows

———

Rainbows don't emerge
From azure skies and brilliant days
But need droplets from storm clouds
To join with sun's resplendent rays

If you leave your eyes wide open
With intent to stay aware
You'll find beauty in the places
Others never stop and stare

———

Please release me from my ego
Take my soul and set it free
And allow me to discover
Who I'm truly meant to be

———

It's time to lay
The past to rest
And venerate what's here
For I'm ready
To live peacefully
Suffused in hope not fear

Keep on planting latent seeds
Give them water, pull the weeds
Then repeat it all again
For we can't be certain when
They'll take root and swiftly grow
Touching lives we'll never know

———

Control is an illusion
For there is no certainty
So let's make life an adventure
Full of possibility

———

Although we may believe
Disaster looms with all hope gone
We must find the strength to forge ahead
And boldly carry on

I choose joy
Not despair
I choose justice
Not unfair
I choose action
Not malaise
I choose resolve
Not praise
I choose kindness
Not disdain
I choose measured
Not insane
I choose life
Not death
I choose hope
With every breath

I must turn darkness
Into light
Resignation
Into fight
Cynicism
Into trust
Underhanded
Into just
Standoffishness
Into heart
Desolation
Into art
Apprehension
Into goal
Agitation
Into soul

Don't lament when one door closes
For another opens wide
Just inviting us to hasten
Toward what's beckoning inside

———

If we never make that brush stroke
Or compose a song's first line
Keep conceptions in our heads
And not convert them to design
If we never lend a hand
To someone struggling in need
Or refuse to take that challenge
Unsure where its path might lead
We will never feel the thrill
Of plunging into life's unknowns
And unleashing our potential
For transformative milestones

There is promise all around us
Yet with wide eyes only seen
For where one finds opportunity
Another heeds routine

———

Our minds are split in two parts
One holds love, the other fear
And our goal is for love's might
To make all darkness disappear

———

Let's delight in every moment
Living blissfully aware
For pure wonder only manifests
With ample time to stare

Memories lodge inside the heart
And not in residential walls
Which is why they'll keep on living
Even if that structure falls

———

Mercy's door is always open
Yet we need to step inside
Leaving pretense at the entry
With intention as our guide

It is not the destination
That determines what you'll see
For pure splendor is wherever
Eyes divulge the mystery

———

If all my wrongs
Were changed to right
If all my darkness
Turned to light
If all my dread
Transformed to hope
I'd surely find
The strength to cope

———

It is not the destination
That determines what you'll see
But the eyes gazing upon it
Wide with possibility

With bended heads
We labor forth
Ensnared in daily strife
Yet so hopelessly
Myopic to
This miracle of life

———

Just abandon what has been
And our erroneous mind story
Moving forward with intent
To live each moment in its glory

When the burden of our lives
Becomes impossible to bear
We must move inside our hearts
Where promise subjugates despair

———

There is nothing
Wrong with Sundays
When you do not
Dread the Mondays

———

Let's manifest our inner light
With freedom to renounce the fight
No longer led astray by fear
For virtue will preside from here

———

If we give ourselves to others
With compassion and pure heart
That intention will keep spreading
Far beyond its humble start

Let's not focus on tomorrow
Or regret transgressions past
But resolve to make this moment
Even better than the last

———

We can't influence our destiny
Or modify the past
So let's venture forth to live each day
As if it were our last

———

Let's live like nothing's looming
Or left lingering behind
And delight in what's before us
Simply manifest to find

Voicing bitterness toward others
Never furthers empathy
For in order to build trust
We cannot judge how others see
Rather honor their perspective
And aspire to understand
That real progress is dependent
On advancing hand in hand

———

The genesis of love and hate
Lies dormant in our soul
Yet requires steadfast nourishment
To manifest control
And we must live ever mindful
To sustain just wholesome seeds
So the others don't transform
Into proliferating weeds

Though we tend to label others
Either villainous or good
We would all prefer performing
Acts of kindness if we could
But too often tribulations
Leave us acting out in ways
Born from adverse circumstances
Prompting punishing malaise
So in knowing both deceit and grace
Flow freely through our veins
We must live inside our hearts
Where utter altruism reigns

———

Just knowing I possess the strength
To drive despair away
Gives me fortitude to battle through
Another grueling day

If we have no expectations
Of how life's supposed to be
Then each day unveils a canvas
To design organically

———

A relentless curiosity
And ever asking why
Is the key to innovation
And transforming what's awry

———

No matter our environs
We can choose the way we see
For our eyes can view the world
As rife with hope or misery

———

If we never leave our comfort zone
Or think outside the box
We'll not find the very key to life
And promise it unlocks

When my heart begins to hammer
And my mind fills with despair
I gaze upward toward the heavens
And repeat this simple prayer

"*I choose life*"

When an outcome goes amiss
Of expectations I desire
Lacking fortitude to meet
The lofty standards I require

"*I choose life*"

When a person I depend on
Breaks my trust and I'm betrayed
Left completely on my own
Suffused in fury and afraid

"*I choose life*"

continues »

When I'm clinging to the past
And fear the future will dawn bleak
Gripped by utter desolation
Scared to hasten forth or speak

"I choose life"

Though I ever may be seeking
A clear answer to the "why"
I now gaze up toward the heavens
Ever bound to boldly cry

"I choose life!"

PRESENCE

Once I saw myself clearly and understood the key to achieving peace was "being present in this moment experiencing _____" I realized I didn't even know what that meant.

I had always been someone who *"lived in her head,"*
offering a profound gift in being able to access my
imagination and the boundless realm of white space
within. This imagination should have provided the ideal
refuge from dark thoughts and sense of hopelessness
ever threatening to submerge me. But being a
"heady individual" also carried the strong impulse to
over-analyze, criticize and intellectualize, making me
anxious, fearful, and continually enmeshed in negative
thought patterns. Questioning why situations weren't
playing out exactly as I envisioned and expected, thus
second-guessing my own and others' actions, brought
me constant anguish, as I was never able to revel in the
moment. Instead, I was either living in the past feeling
guilty over what should have been, bitter over how
others had hurt me long ago, or worrying about the
future and strategizing how I would control/change/
avoid or respond to what I anticipated occurring. I
was never truly experiencing life in my heart. And
during periods when I wasn't in my imagination or head
challenging, churning and analyzing, I was drowning
in malaise at the bottom of my gut, wallowing in fear
of mortality and life's futility. However, once I saw
myself clearly and understood the key to achieving
peace was *"being present in this moment experiencing
life,"* I realized I didn't even know what that meant. The
endless mind-loop of uncertainty, analysis and negativity
never brought solace or freedom, leaving me burdened,
exhausted and depressed.

I had spent an entire lifetime engaged in continual activity to quiet the drumbeat of mortality. Without even understanding why, I had filled every moment blindly racing to experience as much as I could— checking goals off a list and engaging in continual motion to feel a sense of accomplishment and purpose. Anything involving movement became my go-to—impelled to buy innumerable baubles to amass a treasure chest of stunning possessions, read every bit of content possible and listen to every podcast available to acquire profound insight, travel far and wide to fill my head with marvelous sights and sounds, and engorge myself with experience so as to never miss out on a life-changing revelation. Yet I now realized always needing more and making life an all-out race held no joy, for I never engaged in activities for the pure elation of doing so. Not to mention, after decades of running I was still deeply troubled with an overwhelming sense of futility, plus so physically and mentally drained I would surely collapse if I didn't ease up. And to be honest, I finally craved nothing more than just slowing down and simply resting where I was.

As I crossed over my fifth decade, sheer exhaustion from years of racing, coupled with midlife hormonal changes unleashing waves of emotion so intense I didn't know what pummeled me, made it impossible to put up familiar barricades of resistance or have energy to elude despair. In fact, I didn't want to fight or harbor anguish another moment, determined to finally accept and embrace all feeling, good or bad. Likewise, I no longer possessed strength to hide from the truth of existence and charge forward filling interminable emptiness with contrived activity, knowing it would be in vain. For buying material objects or engaging in useless, frenetic motion weren't going to answer my deeper questions or bring acceptance over how and what I was feeling. And most unfortunately, I finally needed to accept despair as part of me without denial, resistance, repression or hope for anything different. That was when I simply stopped fighting and surrendered to the pain, turning my face toward the heavens and crying, *"I give up—do what you want with me!"* Instead of skirting terror, I finally let it submerge me, determined to stare it in the eye. However, I was so accustomed to either resisting or repressing negative feelings, or instinctively seeking solace through action to avoid overwhelming emotions, I was entirely ill-equipped to withstand the desolation now suffusing me. And yet, I knew the only way to move forward was to remain entrenched in misery and not attempt escape.

Meeting despair and touching the bleakness of mortality shook me to such an extent my desire for control against that feeling instinctively kicked in. And before I knew what was happening, I became rabidly obsessed with an even more extreme and rigid form of doing, utterly desperate to make meaning

This meant living at the juncture of what I most enjoyed doing and what I was best equipped to excel in, since only in that space did I have the greatest opportunity to be of true service and make a real difference while on Earth.

during my remaining years. This all began with a realization emerging as the odd yet firm contention: *"I will never make another pair of earrings,"* since having visited despair I needed to stop wasting time engaged in frivolous pastimes and immediately make the most of life. This meant living at the juncture of what I most enjoyed doing and what I was best equipped to excel in, since only in that space did I have the greatest opportunity to be of true service and make a real difference while on Earth. Suddenly, all random, pleasurable activity squandering hours but not creating immortal meaning seemed totally senseless. I had plainly wasted decades running frenetically from destination to destination to drown out the sound of my internal ticking clock, engaging in frivolity to superficially fill the void and mask despair. In fact, the more panicked I became the more I felt the desperate need to run faster and create further in a futile race to nowhere, avoiding the truth of who I was and what I felt deepest in my soul. And since I was now fortunate to have honed in on my sweet spot, anything diverting me from that path was pointless. It was the clearest and most focused I had ever been in my life.

I suddenly envisioned taking stock during my final days and knew I would never be remembered for scoring another fashion bargain, watching another reality series, listening to another inspirational podcast, and most of all making more earrings, which I enjoyed immensely although my creations were those of a novice and by no means works of art. However, despite the fact that making earrings and other trivial pastimes brought me pleasure, I now believed they were a waste of precious time and purely masking despair. They were not my unique path to leaving a legacy and impacting others. I would never make a pair of earrings touching someone more than thousands of beautiful pairs they could purchase elsewhere, but had a greater chance of impacting them through the words and toys so naturally forged from anguish. I would therefore keep myself submerged in pain creating directly out of it, preventing myself from rising and engaging in contrived activity to artificially lift my spirits.

This behavior stemmed from the conviction that if all activity didn't lead to superior invention, then it made no sense engaging in it, even if joyful. Taken to the extreme, it became horribly sadistic and drove me to the brink of madness in denying myself the ability to experience pleasure. Making earrings signified super-fluous, non-transformational creation now deemed unworthy, which quickly moved to defining any form of pleasure as masking reality and absolutely forbidden. Once again, I had become so intent on leaving a legacy and demanding, needing and formalizing purpose that I was substituting joy with rabid creation. And now, more than ever before, was channeling torrents of lifelong, existential angst into perfection in demanding brilliant performance and copious results from all artistic endeavors.

In disallowing myself to feel hope or gratification, I prohibited activity with potential to extricate me from despair. I ceased reading, watching television, crafting, searching the internet and physical stores for new product ideas, listening to music, eating satiating foods (restricting my diet even further by limiting the hours in which I ate and no longer consuming carbohydrates), and purchasing aesthetically pleasing jewelry or articles of clothing. In fact, before long I suppressed *any* sense of desire or promise. Since life was going to end in despair, I might as well stay suffused in truth and avoid escaping, for it was misleading to delude myself with meaningless, manufactured activity when darkness would soon descend with all hope gone. And experiencing hope would only entice me to crave its continuation.

However, my existence soon plummeted into such darkness that I knew I would end my life before punishing myself further and drowning in this toxic hell. I longed to experience joy and embrace laughter without clinging, but didn't know how to do so when the fall from pleasure back to nothingness would be unbearable. Yet in truth, I was so familiar with feeling and fighting pain I found it somewhat reassuring, although simultaneously desperate for release from its grip. For when I was deep in the throes of anguish I felt

calm, knowing nothing bad could befall me since it was
already occurring; yet whenever I felt joy, was fearfully
looking over my shoulder waiting for doom to descend,
knowing pain was ever lurking. Hence joy was ultimately
a letdown, whereas pain brought no letdown and was
what I expected and deserved. That said, I couldn't
eternally deny myself pleasure, for I loved nothing more
than reveling in nature's beauty and finding marvels
within its depths, looking forward to special occasions,
eating delicious food and savoring every morsel, enjoying
relaxing vacations with loved ones, and delighting in
the hard fought achievements of family and friends.
However, I couldn't cling to pleasurable experiences
once they passed, aware I must remain unwavering
no matter the circumstance. Whether feeling anger,
sadness, joy or frustration, I needed to experience those
emotions exactly as they were, but then allow them to
pass through without grasping. In fact, maintaining
steadfast composure would be my ultimate control! For
I would *always* have a range of emotions and thoughts
going forward, but had complete autonomy over whether
or not I allowed them to spark disturbance or desire. I
later learned that the word for this is *equanimous*, and
embracing it has become my abiding intention.

One of my big realizations was that being equanimous
didn't mean I wasn't able to experience a full gamut of
feelings, since I originally feared being non-reactive
meant I needed to remain objectively in the middle,

never traveling to emotional highs or lows. And honestly, I could never live life neutrally in the middle, for a life of tempered feeling wasn't living at all, even if the only method of attaining inner peace. It rather entailed allowing every emotion to flow in and out, just not clinging to them and craving pleasurable experiences to lift me back up. I likened it to the weather—reveling in those perfect spring or fall days eager to spend every moment outdoors basking in the beauty, then awakening the next morning to gloomy, stormy conditions. That didn't mean I couldn't wholeheartedly enjoy beautiful days, I just couldn't be disappointed when storms came and equally resolved to accept those as well.

In order to move forward I needed to live in my heart experiencing life, while reframing the story in my head to one of possibility. My overarching mission was now to derive meaning from a combination of: 1) creating from internal angst, 2) helping others find light in the throes of angst, and 3) openly and confidently engaging in mutually loving relationships. I had the first point covered, but since I was terrified of forging relationships, needed to disregard the temperature of the water and just dive in, embracing whatever greeted me once I hit the surface. For I was no longer able to function as a robotic, soulless vessel continually serving others without expressing feelings and developing reciprocal connections.

I needed to give myself permission to authentically create, as that was my reason for living and intoxicated me like nothing else.

Every molecule of my being desired autonomy to exist honestly and create organically no matter the outcome. I had suffered too long with trying to make myself and every emerging product perfect and never succeeding. I thus needed to give myself permission to authentically create, as that was my reason for living and intoxicated me like nothing else. And one evening, in the midst of my pleasure anorexia, I was driving home with the windows down and music playing, and felt the summer breeze lift the hair back from my face. It was a flash of sheer abandonment, and for the first time in months, my mind and body remained simultaneously still. And I suddenly realized, *"I just want to make a pair of earrings this very moment,"* stunned that the innate passion to create arose from pure, unabashed longing. In fact, that hunger was so sincere and intense that I was left reeling, finally throwing myself before the ruthless inner demon and begging it to simply create whatever my heart desired. Likewise, I also realized the extent to which I had been denying myself joy, since all I had ever wanted was to make a simple pair of earrings. And yet, I had cruelly refused that basic pleasure and so many others for what now seemed an eternity.

My empowerment came from the ability to genuinely create without outsider or inner demon defining what to conceive or evaluating the caliber of the output. Forging freely without grade or judgment was my antidote to hopelessness and despair—the only means of wresting order from chaos to derive meaning. For in truth, all

I sought was permission
to move beyond futile
ruminations and
spontaneously invent, now
certain that was the key to
attaining absolute peace.
It was thus imperative to
live in my heart and the
present, not my head and
past or future, expressing
earnestly throughout my
remaining days.

Forging freely without grade or judgment was my antidote to hopelessness and despair—the only means of wresting order from chaos to derive meaning.

A cloud cannot eclipse the sky
Or leaf topple a tree
No ridge harnesses the mountain
Or wave tames the fickle sea
Grief will not erase past misdeeds
Or hope alter destiny
So let's just embrace each moment
And allow all else to be

We're all racing toward the future
Or left grieving miles behind
Planning what will come tomorrow
Or by prior wrongs defined
Yet in spurning what is present
We forsake the chance to see
All the wonder right before us
Born of this reality

Our lives play out on a stage
From birth until that final breath
Just a drama boasting acts
Replete with love, hope, pain and death
And perceiving each new scene
As simply theater with a cast
Will allow its twists and turns
To leave us dazzled yet steadfast

There's no reason to keep running
And explore the next frontier
When the answers we've been seeking
Are already waiting here

———

Courage abounds
When we're willing to stay
And embrace how we feel
Versus running away

———

When will we come to realize
That our savior's not out there
But is waiting in our souls
Once we grow mindfully aware

We don't need our death to end
The pain and turmoil of today
Just to shift all focus inward
And release will come as may

———

What's not channeled into consciousness
Will come to us as fate
Which is why we must dive inward
And set all our bygones straight

We can't think our way to solace
For it's never in the mind
That we access what's imprisoned
Deep within our hearts to find

———

We must see things as they are
Not how the mind wants them to be
For reality's much sweeter
Than an idle fantasy

———

Let's stop searching on the outside
For what's only found within
Since until we know ourselves
The search for truth cannot begin

Ever hurtling toward tomorrow
Masks the wonder here today
Since we'll only find fulfillment
With a willingness to stay

———

My body's truly yearning
To stop moving and stand still
With the fortitude to access
My potential to fulfill

I'll never be at peace until
The racing stops and I stand still
To hear my soul's impassioned cry
With no compulsion to deny

———

Until we stop resisting
Fully present in this place
We'll remain forever searching
Running life's insipid race

———

I understand awareness
Calls for slackening my pace
With a willingness to exit
This interminable race

We emerge as undivided
From earth's every living thing
Wholly grounded in each moment
With no urge to want or cling
But then soon begin believing
That we need to strive for more
With that ardent misconception
Making life a constant war
And before long joy is gone
Leaving us anxious and depressed
As the freedom we once knew
Becomes entirely suppressed
With our time then spent discarding
Pretense worn throughout the years
To reclaim just who we were
Before youth bowed to ego's fears

All I ever wanted
Was to matter and be seen
Which propelled me on a journey
To define what life would mean
With continual achievement
As the measure of success
But that never brought me closer
To attaining happiness
When at last I came to realize
That it takes remaining still
To discover inner purpose
And my destiny fulfill

Who am I with no presumption
Of how life's supposed to be
With no urgency to battle
And defeat mortality
With no want, hope or illusion
Liberated from the quest
Bound to savor every moment
Granting misery a rest
Who am I with nothing absent
Wholly ground in love not fear
I am just a simple being
Truly grateful to rest here

Stop lamenting the past
For that die has been cast
And let's treasure today
To be all that it may

———

It is not until we move forth
With intention to just be
That we'll live each day in consciousness
Not reactivity

———

You can choose to be a victim
Blaming others for your plight
Or start living with intention
To make every moment bright

We stand awestruck atop mountains
And gaze spellbound at the sea
Treasure verdant woodland trails
And praise a sunset's majesty
Then behold the starlit sky
And savor blossoms fresh with dew
Yet don't ever stop to marvel
At our own resplendent view

———

I contemplate what should have been
Or what awaits ahead
Left imprisoned by uncertainty
And wallowing in dread
Ever longing to be present
To the wonder waiting here
Freely soaring with abandon
To live life in hope not fear

Although our mind
Spends years confined
Lamenting what's to be
Our true essence
Yearns for presence
And to idle peacefully

———

If intention's fully present
Utter freedom isn't far
For believing what we need to be
Will lead to who we are

———

It is not the destination
But the sights along the way
Which awaken us to wonder
And secure us in today

Who we brandish to the world
Is just a concept of the mind
For the essence of our spirit
Isn't easily defined

———

Our essence takes up residence
Within a rigid frame
To endure a lifetime captive
Victim of the ego game

———

Our essence cannot be defined
Which isn't pleasing to the mind
That needs to label and control
And hold us captive in a role

———

If our essence is eternal
Yet imprisoned in a shell
Then death shouldn't be resisted
But a portal out of hell

When I slow down
Intent to "be"
No solace washes
Over me
Instead the fears
Come surging through
Provoking panic
To ensue
But now resolved
On standing still
With no objective
To fulfill
Allow the angst
To drown my soul
Arousing dread
I can't control

If we revel in this moment
Life's potential will arise
For it's only deep in stillness
We may come to realize
All the answers we've been seeking
Were inside us from the start
Though not accessed in the head
But navigated through the heart

———

I am just a simple being
Fully present in the now
Here to savor every moment
And no feeling disallow

———

If we face our raging tempest
Holding steadfast till its end
We'll develop the resilience
That allows us to transcend

Until our sense of self
Moves from the mind into the heart
We will never find connection
And remain our lives apart

———

I need to live in presence
Not imprisoned miles away
Helpless hostage of cognition
Bound by rampant thought each day
For the years will swiftly hasten
With my life just passing by
And I'll miss out on what mattered
Never understanding why

———

All the seeds of understanding
Wait unconscious in our being
Till our earnest introspection
Lets them thrive into what's freeing

We are not the things that happen
But the ones they happen to
For they're nothing more than waves
On the vast ocean inside you

———

Our minds incite the storms
That mask the sun's effulgent rays
While our beings are the sun itself
Still shining through dark days

"If only" are two words
That must be banned from conversation
For regretting serves no purpose
When today is our salvation

———

No problem to solve
No guilt to absolve
No onus to do
No struggling through
No casting of blame
No cringing in shame
Now able to be
Simply genuine me

———

Happiness must not become
Life's fundamental goal
But arise from finding purpose
And contentment in our soul

You will only find yourself
And be relieved of all desire
If you strive for nothing more
Than diving in to rocket higher

———

Why should I be so mind-full
And not strive to be mind-less
When my brain is filled with darkness
And provokes such deep distress!

I contact grace
Within the space
Alive inside my chest
That expands into
A world anew
Each time I stop and rest

———

I lost decades racing forward
Blindly focused on the goal
With continual achievement
The elixir to feel whole
But it turned out my performance
Didn't stem despair within
Only presence in the moment
Let awakening begin

———

When we realize there's a difference
Between sentiments and facts
We'll not heed our foolish brain
That just continually reacts

It takes a steadfast practice
To remember what is good
So we don't become fixated
On the adverse likelihood
Thereby deepening awareness
Of life's blessings all around
Will help cultivate true gratitude
And promise to abound

———

Why am I so afflicted
By results I can't control
Wishing outcomes could be molded
Into manufactured goal
Yet unable to affect
Conclusions never mine to sway
Means releasing all attachment
Still remains the only way

The seasons change
And time rolls by
At such a rapid pace
I am desperate
To step off the track
Since life is not a race
And these decades
Spent in motion
Haven't soothed this restless soul
Thereby living
In the moment
Now remains my utmost goal

We can walk a path one hundred times
Without a second thought
For it won't be fathomed differently
Or offer wisdom sought
Till the power of awareness
Grants lucidity of seeing
All the wonder ever-present
And the joy of wholly being

———

No existence of past sorrows
Will shed darkness on today
When rejoicing in this moment
Keeps all history at bay

———

We are no thing
And yet all things
Simple beings
In this space
Left to cherish
Every moment
Once there's nothing
More to chase

Since a focus on the outcome
Leaves us anxious and depressed
We must use this present moment
As the path to happiness

———

No one knows the price I pay
For living with this mind
I would gladly trade it any day
If only peace I'd find

———

If our problems are illusions
And our worries in the mind
Then as soon as we stop thinking
Pain will cease and peace we'll find

Living bound by expectation
Leaves us bitter and depressed
For events so rarely play out
As we ever would have guessed
And our days must be permitted
To organically unfold
Celebrating every moment
With its marvels to behold

—

Can't race ahead
Or lag behind
For then we'll never see
All the wonder
Right before us
Rife with possibility

Let's relinquish the past
Since regrets cloud the way
And inhibit the mind
From embracing today

———

With no intent to rush
We can revel in the hush
That arises when we stay
In the promise of today

When we race around frenetically
Time marches right on by
So addicted to accomplishment
Yet never asking why
We obsess about tomorrow
With no willingness to see
Every moment is a portal
To pure possibility

———

Rushing headlong through our lives
Leaves little respite to stand still
So dependent on accomplishment
Unlikely to fulfill
Since it's not until we pause
With eyes amenable to see
That each moment reigns eternal
And awash in mystery

Feel the breath that calmly rests
Within the stillness of the soul
For it's there we'll find contentment
Without chasing gain or goal

———

How I long for a vacation
From the tumult of my mind
For I cannot spend another day
By futile thoughts confined

———

The space between what is
And what our minds believe should be
Means we haven't yet accepted
What is waiting presently

Why do we leave our bodies
When they know just what to do
How to learn, love, laugh and sing
Plus even dance the whole night through
To take refuge in our heads
Enmeshed in fear and misery
Disconnected from awareness
And sincere affinity

———

My tendency had always been
To flee from life down here
Seeking sanctum in the heavens
Where abandon conquered fear
When the pathway to fulfillment
Meant remaining in one place
Where affinity to others
Forged true everlasting grace

Pain and pleasure are the waves
Upon a sea of consciousness
While our souls remain serene
Immune to surges and distress

———

We will surely know great pleasure
To be savored while it's here
Then must simply let it pass
Remaining severed from all fear

———

An eternal, vibrant being
Lies within this aging hide
Seeking oneness with the cosmos
And in stillness to reside

When will we stop believing
That a prince will come along
And our lives flow like a fairy tale
With forest friends in song
For we cannot seek from others
What is only found within
And the fantasy must end
Before our memoir can begin

We must spend our lifetimes being
And abandon constant doing
With our eyes intent on seeing
Not perpetually pursuing

———

Why do our minds and bodies
Spend their years a world apart
With the head adrift in space
And disconnected from the heart?

———

When we leave the heart behind
Enmeshed in thought a world above
We grow wholly isolated
By beliefs that hinder love

Blind achievement is exhausting
While intention knows no stress
For a clarity of purpose
Births eternal happiness

———

We believe big roles and titles
Will enable our success
For they offer validation
And a sense of happiness
But they're simply a distraction
From the work we're called to do
Which takes vanquishing the self
And diving inward for what's true

If you take a breath and revel
In embracing what is here
You will see there really wasn't
Much of anything to fear

———

Though blue skies are always waiting
Right above the murky gray
The real key to life is staying
Wholly steadfast either way

———

Contentment can't be found
From forms that dissipate and die
Rather only in our beings
Once we bid all else goodbye

Just surrender the skin
And allow what's within
To release and let go
Into larger life flow

————

In the quietude of mind
We simply access all that's true
Yet the only way to enter
Is dissolving all we do
For the moment we stop racing
And investigate our fear
We'll awaken to the promise
Ever manifesting here

————

If we spend our lifetimes questioning
And ever asking why
We'll neglect to see the wonder
That beholds the naked eye

The wisdom we are seeking
Is enshrouded deep within
Just awaiting utter presence
For its teachings to begin

———

What's perceived in pure awareness
And unmoved by want or fear
Sparks the only truth we know
Impelled to venerate what's here

No more do–er
Just be-er
Now living
Much free-er

———

I will honor dissolution
As the solace for my soul
And accept just simply being
An observer absent role

———

If we venture to define ourselves
By manufactured role
We won't ever be at peace
To live absolved of its control

Ever focused on controlling
That which changes constantly
Leaves us hindered from enjoying
What it truly means to be

———

We have nothing to do
And no places to go
So let's honor what's true
Without living for show

———

If we silence the world's clamor
With our minds completely clear
We'll be able to gaze inward
And discover why we're here

The contentment we are seeking
Is already waiting here
Once we sanctify the moment
And relinquish what we fear

———

If we let our lifelong grip
On accomplishment to slip
Into living life right here
Would this anguish disappear?

———

We must revel in quiescence
For it's only absent sound
We'll discover true intention
Flush with freedom to expound

———

In the grip of competition
And forever wanting more
We will never be at peace
To access what we're searching for

When angst pronounced "I'm here to stay
And not about to leave"
I felt utterly despondent
Sorely needing a reprieve
From the unrelenting terror
That suffused my fragile soul
For the shackles of despair
Had me imprisoned by control
Yet soon came to learn malaise
Lived in the head and not the heart
And although the darkness
Never would conclusively depart
I could choose to greet each moment
Finding promise in what's here
For supplanting dread with presence
Rendered nothing left to fear

I wish to lose my mind
For without it I will find
All the wonder waiting here
Without destiny to fear

———

Say goodbye to the trance
Of habitual dance
And emerge into seeing
The wonder in being

———

Keeping silent in the mind
And contemplative in the heart
Is the only way to realize
We were perfect from the start

In the mirror of awareness
Only one reflection shines
Just the truth of your pure self
Though veiled as long as it defines

———

Don't leave latent notes unwritten
Or auspicious stones unturned
Don't leave idle words unstated
Or past traveled bridges burned
Wholly revel in each moment
Free to dance, laugh, love and sing
Firmly rooted in compassion
And imbibing life's wellspring

I was running from the demons
Searching for a place to hide
When there wasn't any fleeing
From what needed love inside

———

We cannot attach our anchors
Onto anything in motion
And must find what stays entrenched
Within our undulating ocean

———

Dissolve into the present
Where each moment dawns anew
And the power of awareness
Is a blossom fresh with dew

I was desperate to escape
The ghastly dungeon of my brain
Bound to find the quickest route
To extricate me from such pain
But no matter where I raced
I couldn't keep the angst at bay
Since I needed to renounce
Beliefs that wouldn't let me stay
For the only way to know
Eternal peace and find what's true
Was to listen to my heart
And take the path directly through

VOLUME TEN

LIBERATION

I had been suffocating under a mountain of flawed perceptions, with each revelation enabling me to shed another fallacy until able to step out as my honest self.

As my armor of self-protection began to slacken,
I experienced a depth of feeling repressed under a
lifetime of inauthenticity. I had been suffocating
under a mountain of flawed perceptions, with each
revelation enabling me to shed another fallacy until
able to step out as my honest self. Through integrating
these disparate pieces, the wall of isolation came
crashing down, and I realized how desperately I craved
acceptance of my innermost fears, hopes and dreams.
Yet having convinced myself finding connection wasn't
possible, I protected myself from doing so, absolutely
terrified of forming relationships and having them fail
or being rejected for who I truly was.

One of the greatest ironies was that *"my people"* had
actually been out there all the time, I had just never
opened myself up to finding them, struggling in
vain to fit in with the socially accepted, extroverted,
superficial ones instead. As I reflected back on my life,
it was clear I had always been drawn to intellectual,
soulful, despairing, introverted types, yet once catching
a glimpse of their inner turmoil went racing in the
opposite direction. For how could I embrace that
sense of desperation and instability in others when I
completely repressed and denied it in myself?

I had always ridiculed, judged and quashed any complex
feeling or person, unaware I was actually rejecting
myself.   In essence, the derision I held toward others
was just self-directed contempt, demanding they treat

me in a manner I had never been able to treat myself.
And how could I expect others to bestow kindness and
respect if I had never manifested and couldn't give them
to myself? The person they knew was a stoic mountain
without wants, needs, feelings or emotions, unworthy
of compassionate treatment. My severe repression
disabled me from feeling empathy toward any one
or thing, with every action manufactured toward an
orchestrated end. And having never conveyed desire
for benevolence or consideration from others, I wasn't
respected for having needs of my own or deserving
of mercy.

Since I was now ready for honest relationships,
the question had become: *how do overly sensitive,
introverted, heady, despairing types ever find their people
if they're lurking in the shadows?* That answer during
my first five decades of life was: *with much difficulty.*
Yet I now understood that was largely because no one
(including myself) knew who the real Melissa even
was. After putting my feelings aside for decades, I had
no idea how I felt and what I believed, or even how to
access those thoughts and feelings. Likewise, my prior
relationships held no meaning, as I never learned how
to forge connections involving personal disclosures,
instead becoming a reactionary martyr. Relationships
never involved my heart—just the same one-sided,
non-emotional pattern—and were therefore ultimately

unfulfilling and expendable. And having never gone out into the world authentically, how could I expect to attract others like me? Yet my newfound awareness helped me to finally comprehend what it meant to connect from a place of authenticity.

This deep yearning for connection ushered in optimism I had never known. I now realized my mission extended well beyond the creation of toys, which had indeed enabled me to channel inner pain, but brought no sense of personal connection with the products' recipients. At long last I felt the dots of my life uniting in an even more fulfilling manner, with every life experience leading in the direction of helping others extricate light from darkness. I had learned firsthand that darkness didn't have to emanate from darkness, and we all had capacity to turn pain into promise. I could use my life experience and encourage others locked in their heads to find a lifeline and purpose through creating, giving to or helping others from the wellspring in their hearts.

My habitual process had always been to over-analyze and intellectualize, becoming immediately enmeshed in negative thought patterns. Another profound realization came in seeing I had been living each day almost entirely in my head, which was fearful, judgmental and pessimistic about human interaction,

entrapped in some combination of: living in the past
lamenting what had been, feeling guilty over actions I
should have taken, steeped in anger over how others
had hurt me, or worrying about the future fearing
what might happen and planning how I would avoid
it and/or respond. I was never truly connecting,
since my head was either recalling fractured former
relationships or fearing what turn a close bond might
take in the future. In order to move forward I needed
to stay out of my head and either live in my heart with
no mind story, or reframe the story in my head to one
of possibility.

I was desperate to exist wholly in my heart connecting
with others and transforming angst into vibrant
content. I therefore needed tangible motivation, which
ultimately became a lifeline, to repeat when I started
overthinking and falling into despair. If I wasn't
deliberate about turning negativity into positivity to
derive meaning, I would operate out of fear, talking
myself out of truly living and never finding purpose
or connection. However, as long as I could take
those innate qualities I so despised—introversion,
introspection, agitation and desperation—and use them
to sincerely connect with others, then my life would
have meaning and my existence would make sense. My
battle cry was now: Step on out of the head moving
into the heart, *free to channel all dread into jubilant art.*

Step on out of the head
moving into the heart,
free to channel all dread
into jubilant art.

Moreover, I needed to protect against falling into the
"why me" mindset, taking measures well in advance to
stay healthy instead of feeling sorry for myself. After
all, this was who I was and I wasn't going to change my
chemical makeup. Thus another critical life lesson was
to accept myself in totality and embrace that with all
my heart, employing a daily practice to remain steadfast
throughout life's ups and downs. I now understood
being Melissa came with both positives and unique
challenges, not necessarily good or bad, just my own
personal reality. And the most significant revelation
arising from accepting myself was in no longer trying
to change into or wishing to be someone else, for I
now knew running from and denying one's true self
only led to inauthenticity, bitterness and ultimately
severe depression.

Understanding I possessed over-excitabilities provided
the first optimistic view of personality traits I had
always perceived as negative. I now understood that my
innumerable challenges and utter sense of hopelessness
were indeed necessary ingredients to personal growth,
emotional development and finding fulfillment.
However, it came down to developing a very tactical life
plan to follow without fail and force my life to matter,
for I alone was maker of personal meaning. It was
so profoundly simple, but dependent on perpetually
creating in my heart and truly living that mantra each
and every day, rather than thinking in my head. Thus
from here on out, I would strive to welcome my true self,

be honest about who I was, open myself up to rejection, and meet others at that juncture as well. This involved offering forgiveness for never listening to or trusting my inner cry, never accepting who I truly was, never honoring my truth, and never manifesting self–love. How ironic that I had been livid at others for neglecting to provide what I was unable to provide myself!

With the newfound knowledge that there were others in the world gripped with despair, I was impelled to share my experience and reveal the path out of darkness no one had ever shown me. For if I could embark on such a journey at this late stage in life, I knew others could do so at much earlier stages in theirs. I needed to encourage them to never let the cry of their inner voices get drowned out by the clamor of the outside world, since denying their truth would impede them from finding purpose and developing their unique potential. Hence my foremost goal was to now help others answer the question: *What gives **your** life true meaning?*

The other astonishing discovery was perhaps I was acting courageously or even defying odds when I fought back against internal malaise and successfully transformed it to positivity. For most individuals, that was no accomplishment in that they woke up hopeful each morning, but I likewise had the same ability to access promise if I fought to do so. Given my internal makeup, finding resolve to rise above inner chaos some days was heroic, however that didn't mean I was weak but rather strong and a fighter. It was a momentous awakening; I was powerful with strength and courage to control my destiny and shape each day without assistance from anyone or anything. It was as if a fire had finally been kindled in my soul.

I also realized I had been waiting my entire life for something that would never happen—hoping everyone would come to their senses bestowing acceptance and validation I desperately craved—when I simply needed to give myself that very love. I had been so bound by expectation, disappointment, and then blaming others for my woes and needing their acknowledgment to make me whole, I neglected to see it only came down to me. In fact, all my energy was channeled into something entirely out of my control and I was letting it define me! And how could I ever change the actions and behaviors of others? Not to mention, it turned out I actually didn't need others to change at all, but simply needed to change my expectations of them and make my own actions consistent with who I truly was, since "*expecting*" left me powerless, disillusioned, confused and bitter, while still desperately seeking.

After five decades of wallowing in self-pity, I knew I could only have expectations for my own behavior and actions. In fact, it turned out I held infinite power right inside me! Whether I chose to live, die, or manifest optimism/hope versus negativity/bitterness was entirely in my control and my choice. That was a critical insight

as I could completely control how I conducted myself
and my reaction to events unfolding before me. For
many years I had controlled how I acted and honestly,
even under a microscope, felt reasonably good about
my conduct. Yet the way in which I responded to
others' behavior was deplorable—becoming either
a spineless victim or petulant child and recoiling in
the face of perceived: 1) mistreatment, 2) criticism of
my actions, or 3) failure to meet my expectations. It
was now imperative to change these misinformed
perceptions and transform this all-consuming sense
of powerlessness and negative mindset making me
depressed and victimized, into positivity. That meant
ensuring I was conducting myself earnestly and then
simply accepting whatever response ensued. However,
I could no longer let those reactions impact me
emotionally, whether positively or negatively.

Although I had now made conscious decisions to
choose life and funnel despair into positivity, those
choices were still only the beginning. I now knew
existential depression couldn't *"be cured,"* and I
wasn't going to *"get better"* from experiencing acute
sensitivities. Similar to anyone living with a chronic
condition or disease, I had a personality condition
needing constant management of its symptoms to
effectively function. If I pretended they didn't exist,
tried to repress or ignore them, or felt angry or defeatist
about my state, the fog would swiftly roll in and I
might never reemerge. I therefore needed to actively

talk myself off the ledge numerous times each day to
survive, and that largely involved not overthinking
in my head. My ego attempted to make it more
complicated, but I simply needed to cease rumination
suffusing me in negativity and fear, since the scenarios
envisioned rarely occurred and yet I exhausted and
depressed myself with crazy anticipations. Whenever
I stopped thinking and turned angst into spontaneous
action and positive creation, I felt exhilarated and
at peace. My head was nothing more than a prison,
actually—a dank, dark cavern and direct channel
to despair.

My final epiphany was that I would never find
fulfillment until the voice most authentically flowing
out of me was embraced by others. Although I was
now over a half century in age, I had still never forged
a genuine relationship in my honest voice. And if my
truth and life experience could finally revel in light
and touch others, it would inextricably link my soul to
humanity far beyond mortal form, granting an eternal
sense of oneness and profound inner peace.

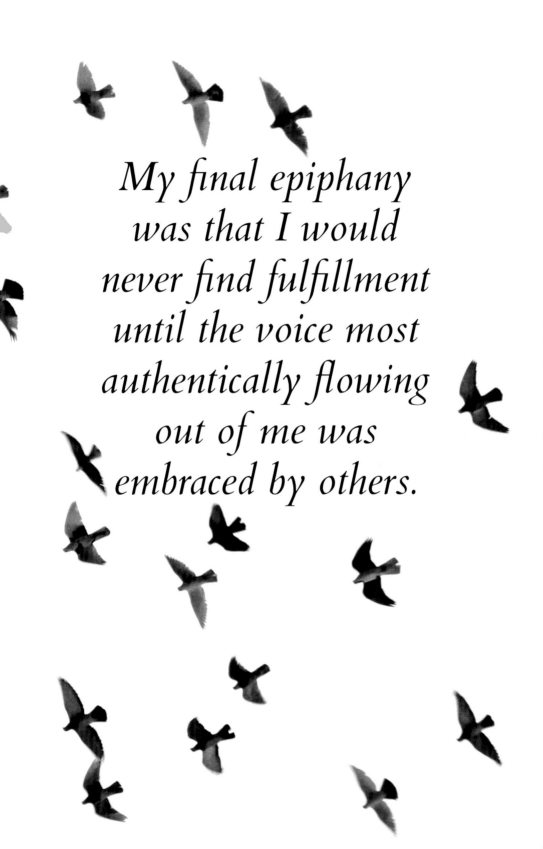

*My final epiphany
was that I would
never find fulfillment
until the voice most
authentically flowing
out of me was
embraced by others.*

A star is no less brilliant
Brightly twinkling in the sky
And a sunrise just as vibrant
With bold hues to greet the eye
Seagulls calls are no less stirring
Heard distinctly as they soar
And the ocean just as mighty
When waves rashly pound the shore
A gardenia is still fragrant
Petals open to the world
And the mountains no less striking
With their magnitude unfurled
So then why do people mask
The way they speak, think, act and feel
When the universe prescribes
A path of unabashed reveal?

I won't even last one day
Bound to a manufactured plan
And must spend my life expressing
As sincerely as I can

———

As one commanded by emotion
Ruled by passion, moved by notion
Wavering from lows to highs
Forsaking peace in others' eyes
But all the while well aware
That even in my worst despair
I'd never as a consequence
Propose a life of temperance

———

You can only be a trail guide
Having walked that path before
Well aware of where it leads
And what the journey has in store...

The way to change the world
Is just to simply change the mind
And believe a different truth
That calls for loving humankind

—

The world was never wrong
Just my beliefs of it as such
And released from past reminders
Am acquitted from their clutch

Condemning is a battle
No one ever really wins
For it's only through compassion
That impunity begins

———

Compassion offers others
The propensity to change
By renouncing past perceptions
With forgiveness in exchange

———

Forgiveness takes a lifetime
And is challenging indeed
Since it takes discarding baggage
To emerge completely freed

———

The only way to heal the past
Is just to let it go
Since it's only through surrender
That we'll ever truly grow

We will never truly love
Until we banish those perceptions
That indoctrinate the mind
And leave us bound by misconceptions

———

An incredible acceptance speech
Should never be our gauge
Rather steadfast dedication
To what brought us to the stage

———

Simply waiting for the future
Will ensure it never comes
For we'll never take the actions
To forge positive outcomes

As long as we keep chasing
Affirmation outwardly
We will never find the love
That wholly sets our spirit free

———

If we truly wish to know
We must allow the mind release
And plunge inward toward the soul
To find ourselves and access peace

———

Surrender is the process
Of unburdening the mind
And existing in the heart
With utter freedom ours to find

True detachment from the mind
Bestows a freedom like no other
And allows us to embrace
The gift of loving one another

———

The sun is always shining
Unaware of dark or night
And once severed from the brain
Our souls will revel in its light

———

I am not you, brain
And your problems aren't mine
So I hope you'll let me be
For in your absence I'm just fine

We mustn't search for love
But move the hazards in the way
Of allowing it to enter
And become our true mainstay

———

If we chose the path of love
We'd live in everlasting peace
For world conflict would resolve
And senseless violence would cease

———

We emerge awash in love
Which over time evolves to fear
And until we shed its armor
Will not find our purpose here

———

Love doesn't ever cling
As just another fleeting thing
Shining far beyond all fear
In the rapture of what's here

The only way to know
That you will always be okay
Is to feel it in your heart
Then strive to live it every day

———

The most precious gifts in life
Can't be detected with the eyes
But must inundate the heart
Which filters substance from the guise

———

Though the body lives in time and space
The spirit lives forever
Which ensures soul will prevail
In immortality's endeavor!

There's no power any greater
Than the light that shines within
But we must choose to embrace it
For its brilliance to set in

———

If we wish to banish darkness
We must shower it with light
If we choose to exile fear
We must transform it with love's might

———

Our greatest gift to others
Is bestowing empathy
On ourselves before we spread that love
And touch humanity

We must focus on the things we have
And not on what we want
For the latter leaves us in a race
When life should be a jaunt

———

Fulfillment doesn't lie
In what we think or what we do
But in kindness toward ourselves
That will encompass others too

———

We must manifest benevolence
To every one we meet
For that kindness may be just the thing
To make their lives replete

———

If we only could be loved
For who we are not what we do
We would live each day in peace
Not spend years searching for what's true

Come right on in
Pull up a chair
I'm here to welcome
You, Despair
Please be my guest
No need to hide
The walls have toppled
Down inside
I get it now
You're here to stay
I'll face the truth
Not run away
Let's venture forth
Akin at last
To heal before
My time has passed

Once we leave behind our misery
And open up our eyes
Every day will dawn a blessing
Filled with intrigue and surprise

———

The happiness we yearn for
Is dependent on our brains
For the moment we stop thinking
Only ecstasy remains

———

There lies a vastness past
The furthest reaches of my mind
Which is where I feel at peace
Suffused in love I've yearned to find

Past the mind there's never suffering
No fear or inner strife
Freed from clinging and resisting
Now awake to flow with life

———

I'm the light beyond the mind
Absolved of fear or definition
Long untethered from desire
Content to "be" without cognition

———

True surrender lies in knowing
There is nothing to give up
Certain everything you need
Exists within to fill your cup

We can't piece ourselves together
Till we've truly come apart
For it takes full dissolution
To repair a broken heart

—

The door that locks us in
Is the same door that lets us out
If we view it as the portal
To explore what we're about

—

To know we've been held hostage
By our overbearing mind
Is the dawn of liberation
From the cage we've been confined

Striving to reach our potential
Leaves us paralyzed today
From the fear of moving forth
With expectation in the way
For we musn't let the ego
Hinder concrete action now
Or we'll never see tomorrow
With its promise to avow

———

In the end
Our only cure
Is to battle
And endure
Finding sanctum
In the sorrows
For they kindle
Bright tomorrows

Surrender to yourself
With every action an expression
Of your undisputed truth
Born from releasing all repression

———

With no sentence in the future
Or indictments from the past
We'll be able to start over
Finding clemency at last

———

We may revel in life's pleasures
Then must simply let them go
And embrace life's woes as treasures
For they're paramount to grow

Needing any one or thing
To make us whole and feel complete
Means we haven't yet discovered
How to make ourselves replete

———

How I long to access peace
Within the stillness of my soul
Never needing any one or thing
To feel completely whole

———

I am desperate to break free
Of the shackles binding me
And release this tortured soul
Ever yearning to be whole

I must tap into the mystery
Of what exists within
To discover my life purpose
And relinquish what has been

———

We must heed the heartfelt message
Of our honest voice within
To reveal the pathway forward
And surrender where we've been

———

You will not begin the healing
Till you open into feeling
What is deepest in your soul
And relinquish all control

I'm held captive in a cage
Overwhelmed by inner rage
Truly desperate to break free
And expose the honest me

———

How I long to find the courage
To release the bars inside
And absolve all past dissension
With no secrets left to hide

———

How I yearn to gain release
From decades shackled by the mind
For there's nothing more depressing
Than a lifetime spent confined

What is that thing you love to do
That wholly makes your heart ring true
And lets your spirit come alive
Awash in time and space to thrive?
What is that thing that's always been
Just desperate to flow from within
That wondrous gift which sets you free
To greet the world authentically?

———

To discover who we are
Means first defining who we're not
And exploring different pathways
To reveal what hits the spot

I don't want to say I'm sorry
I don't want to bear this shame
I don't want to need so desperately
To play the victim game
I don't want to act so guilty
I don't want to seem so small
I don't want to focus on their words
Unsure what might befall
I just want to find acceptance
I just want to truly feel
I just want to voice ideas
And show others I'm for real

———

I wish you sorrow
Wish you pain
With years spent thinking
Life's in vain
I wish you envy
Wish you fear
For past them dawn
Salvation here

I'll refuse
To drown in sorrow
I'll no longer
Writhe in pain
I'll avoid
Seething with anger
I'll ignore
My tangled brain
I'll renounce
Playing the victim
I'll resist
The urge to blame
I'll refrain
From second-guessing
I'll cease
Wallowing in shame
I'll accept
That I'm imperfect
I'll concede
I can't control
I'll stay focused
On the journey
To connect
This severed soul

At long last I've come to find
All the demons in my mind
Shan't be battled or disgraced
But wholeheartedly embraced
For once welcomed here to stay
Lose control and slink away

———

We repress our inner voice
Because it speaks so poignantly
In demanding we renounce
A life of strict complacency
For the road to understanding
Is a brambled path indeed
Fraught with trials and tribulations
For alone we must proceed
To our ultimate salvation
In revealing what rings true
Since that heartfelt cry will lead us
To a joy we never knew

I always feared
Being seen as weird
But finally have learned
To love my quirks
Despite the jerks
Who'd rather have me spurned

———

I've no willingness to play
Their selfish, hedonistic game
When the rules by which I vie
Will surely never be the same

———

To embark on self-discovery
Takes fortitude unknown
Yet preferred above the ignorance
That renders hearts alone

Every moment brings potential
To create ourselves anew
With the freedom to discover
What we're truly meant to do

——

Please know right where you stand
Is where you're truly meant to be
For the universe designs
Our path to reach autonomy

——

Chasing avaricious pleasures
May beget brief happiness
But it's only through adversity
We'll realize true success

You can only be a force of change
Once change begins in you
For in learning how to save yourself
You'll rescue others too

———

The moment of surrender
Is when consciousness begins
For we'll find we're not alone
And unanimity's what wins

———

Compassion casts a halo
That illuminates the face
Turning ordinary features
Into renderings of grace

For years I let them take my voice
And tell me what I thought
Since it seemed I hardly had the right
To speak up though I ought
But then gradually amassed the strength
To free the force inside
And transcend fear to assert myself
No longer meant to hide
Now alive with aspiration
Promise rings with every word
For at last I've found my purpose
And a reason to be heard

———

Let all others lead their own lives
While the shift begins in you
Since alone must we endeavor
To our final rendezvous

———

We're all longing for connection
Yet the work we need to do
Is to journey deep inside
And individually break through

If I realized I had months to live
What would my next steps be
Well, for one I'd let all pretense go
To live authentically
For two I'd drop all worry
And abandon needless fear
Moved to treasure every moment
Wholly grateful to be here
For three I'd end all racing
With incessant activity
To find pleasure in just being
Not deny mortality
And for four I'd stop reacting
To what others did and said
Just embrace their inner essence
Choosing empathy instead
For five I'd stop regretting
The transgressions of the past
And accept that I'm imperfect
Fully freed from guilt at last

continues »

For six I'd come to honor
There is no real certainty
And surrender need for order
Living life contentedly
For seven I'd stop trying
To change others through control
And embrace them as they stand here
As true equals absent role
For eight I'd stop believing
I could change my final fate
Now surrendered to rest easy
And each day appreciate
For nine I'd stop rejecting
Ties with friends and family
Now resolved to spend my time
Enjoying loved ones' company
And lastly I'd stop crying
To the powers high above
With the courage to accept myself
And manifest pure love

Attempting introspection
Is quite difficult for those
Scared to look inside their hearts
For fear of what they might expose

———

If we truly seek transcendence
We must honor letting go
For salvation only dawns
Is disavowing all we know

———

If we knew that all our suffering
Would further true elation
Then we'd cherish all our woes
Instead of craving their cessation

If you strive
To reach the stars
Yet still neglect
To pierce the clouds
The sheer courage
Shown in trying
Floats you miles
Above the crowds

———

We each possess a gift
Birthed deep inside us from the start
Though unwrapping it requires
Utter presence in the heart
For the key to life is learning
How to sow our precious seed
Into genuine expression
That sustains the love we need

My facade is ever crumbling
Yet my soul flows forth renewed
Truly bursting with intention
And wholehearted gratitude

———

Please embrace me in my vastness
Fully conscious of my might
For I'm wholly radiating
The full wattage of my light

———

When we're thankful for the blessings
Present every single day
All that gratitude bestowed
Attracts more miracles our way

Banish any one or thing
That doesn't honor who you are
For without a cheering section
We will never get too far

———

I emerged a jigsaw puzzle
Pieces scattered everywhere
Simply longing for connection
As my shield against despair
Yet the kinship I so needed
Was unable to begin
While my feelings were imprisoned
In a cavern deep within
Till at last I found the courage
To release my fragile soul
And I swelled with newfound union
As my puzzle became whole

I am a mighty oak tree
With leaves outstretched toward the sky
Oft endangered by the elements
That rage then roll on by
My appendages are brittle
Yet my trunk stands tall and sound
Ever knowing it's safeguarded
With roots firmly in the ground

———

Most days I wake so fearful
And consumed with utter dread
I'm obliged to seek asylum
In the confines of my bed
Yet resist this inner edict
To fall victim to despair
And command myself to forge ahead
As if I've not a care

If the world is what we make it
Then let's make it utter bliss
Free of wants, needs and desires
Since they forge such emptiness

———

Let's stop wallowing in pity
And complaining "woe is me"
But unfurl those nimble wings
To soar beyond our misery

———

We are perfect here and now
Demanding nothing to be whole
For salvation is within us
And the one thing we control

I'm no longer saying sorry
I'm no longer feeling shame
I'm no longer trying desperately
To play this phony game
I'm no longer acting guilty
I'm no longer staying small
I'm no longer caring what they say
So fearful of them all
I'm embracing imperfection
I'm affirming how I feel
I'm accepting my emotions
Ever striving to be real

Once I shattered the illusion
Life would never be the same
Knowing everyone around me
Was a player in the game
And the ground on which I rested
Crumbled right beneath my feet
Leaving nothing to sustain me
But the sound of my heartbeat

———

I won't resist
Or reprimand
And let all feeling flow
I won't affirm
What's good or bad
And let all clinging go
I won't deny
The way I feel
And welcome failure too
I won't protect
My fragile heart
And honor all that's true

I dove headfirst off a mountain
With no thing to brace my fall
Having finally relinquished
Grasping anything at all

———

We must focus on ourselves
And not on fixing all the rest
For we'll only impact others
When we offer them our best

———

It takes courage to embrace
Who you were truly meant to be
When the world gives no ovation
For expressing honestly

Let's share the truth
That life's a mess
With envy, fear
And emptiness
With years spent lost
Suffused in shame
Tormented by
The need to blame
Let's share these truths
Until they're known
And never bear
Our pain alone

No longer the victim
No longer the show
No longer the will
Of an untamed ego
No longer the masking
No longer the shame
No longer the fury
Of needing to blame
No longer the martyr
No longer the fear
No longer the hurdles
My pathway is clear

I'm dueling death
With every breath
Determined to survive
And end the race
Free to embrace
Each moment I'm alive

———

I'm exhausted
From a lifetime
Chasing answers far and wide
When I simply
Should have stayed at home
And journeyed deep inside

———

I was yearning for connection
Truly desperate to belong
When the love I had been seeking
Was inside me all along

It was only when I paused
And heard the beating of my heart
That I realized all I needed
Was inside me from the start

———

I was yearning for approval
From the others in my life
Always desperate to be seen
As a good mother, friend and wife
But that never proved enough
To aptly fill the gaping hole
And demanded self-compassion
To sustain my barren soul

I was seeking confirmation
From those too consumed to care
Which engendered utter hopelessness
With decades of despair
Till I realized validation
Shan't be found externally
But emerges once we grant ourselves
Wholehearted empathy

———

Phoenix rises
From the ashes
To transcend
Life's brutal gashes
Soaring past
The status quo
In the bliss
Of freedom's glow
Disengaged
From rank or role
Now empowered
By the soul

I relied upon outsiders
To appease this barren soul
Till I learned to love myself
And simply filled the gaping hole

———

To disparage and condemn
Keeps us looking out at them
When it's gazing deep inside
That reveals our steadfast guide

———

Disengage from senseless worry
And resign yourself to fate
Free to access liberation
In a wholly conscious state

At the dawn of liberation
Is dispassion and detachment
For it's there we'll soar above
Our endless yearning for attachment

———

What is life and who are we
Without our memories
Just a canvas with no palette
Or a forest absent trees
Garbled words with no arrangement
Errant notes without a tune
Or perhaps a stagnant ocean
With no waves to pound the dune
Yet if only lost cognition
Brought eternal peace at last
No fixation on the future
Or resistance to the past
Liberated from the ego
With asylum from mind's storm
Ever-present in vast oneness
Love transcending shape and form

How I wish we never listened
To what others thought or said
For they fill us with self-doubt
Left ruminating in our head
Rather living in our hearts
Exploring who we're meant to be
Taking risks and chasing passions
Till our own voice set us free

———

How I long to find release
From caring what they do or say
When unworthiness will cease
And I won't question yesterday
How I long to find release
From all distress of the unknown
With my head and heart at peace
To rest completely on their own

I would scale the tallest mountain
And traverse the widest sea
To find someone who embraces
Who I am authentically

———

I just focused on the package
And denounced the self within
Certain only in appearance
Would I triumph and fit in
Yet it wasn't till I learned
To love the one I was inside
That I realized self-acceptance
Is the greatest form of pride

When the truth of who we are
Becomes entirely enough
We won't covet validation
Or need superficial stuff

———

When you love yourself
And nothing more
Distinctions forfeit meaning
For the love
Of one and all
Resounds in sonorous convening

———

Why squander time
Playing someone else's song
When to write your own concerto
Means you'll solo all life long?

To confront my desperation
I dove into the abyss
Where a channel to awakening
Transcended emptiness

———

It was only when my anguish
Grew impossible to bear
I resolved to stop resisting
And surrendered to despair

———

Do not run from despair
Or fall victim to pain
Never hide from the truth
Sensing all is in vain
Face the terror head-on
Stare it straight in the eye
And don't ever back down
Till the moment you die

I feel blessed
No longer cursed
For I'm rash
And unrehearsed
Proudly venting
Raw emotion
Raging stormy
Like the ocean
Soaring higher
Than the stars
Baring all
My grisly scars
Living distant
From the herd
Now a bold
Unfettered bird

It is only when we share
Just who we are and how we feel
That we'll truly find connection
With our hearts absolved to heal

———

I have such a fervent appetite
To set myself apart
And ascend above the masses
To express what's in my heart

———

Keep on going
Don't look back
And lift your head up high
Share the truth
Of who you are
And feel love's passion unify
Don't lament
What might have been
Or prior yearnings left behind
But stay present
In this moment
With the joy now yours to find

If I should fall victim to some malady
That causes my life to just end suddenly
Please trust that I loved every one of you so
With a passion beyond what you ever will know
While the joys in my life have been fleeting at best
You all radiate light which now guides me to rest
And absolved is at last where in peace I will be
Watching down with such pride at my bright legacy
Make the most of your wonderful gifts through the pain
And remember the sun always shines after rain

Love has been here waiting
To receive with open arms
We just haven't paused to greet it
Chasing folly and its charms

———

My body is dissolving
As my soul begins evolving
Now untethered from all form
With love's power to transform

———

We must cultivate our gardens
To grow vibrantly alive
Then disperse the fertile seeds we've sown
And help the world to thrive

———

We must offer absolution
For aspersions wrongly cast
Or we'll spend our lives imprisoned
By transgressions of the past

We all deserve redemption
For the misdeeds we have done
Knowing even barren wastelands
Will still flourish in the sun

———

My life will not have meaning
Nor this misery subside
Till my story touches others
And I've nothing left to hide

———

Please embrace me as I stand here
Not as one you'd like to see
For I need to be accepted
As I am authentically

———

Since I cannot change how others think
Or what they say and do
I must manifest integrity
And let the rest ensue

When I'm wallowing in pity
And left reeling from the pain
It is clear that I alone
Can choose to extricate my brain
By employing the elixir
That has saved me in the past
Since I've always held the key
To access solace unsurpassed
For my ultimate salvation
In not knowing what will be
Is to boldly keep creating
Throughout life's uncertainty

I've been struggling a lifetime
To emblazon my true path
Living shrouded in pretension
And subdued by others' wrath
Yet still better late than never
For at last I've found my way
Certain every grueling step
Has made me who I am today

Whenever mind and body
Find communion in one place
We will swell with sacred presence
That transcends life's futile race

———

The more I raced frenetically
The emptier I grew
As I needed to find solace
Gazing inward for what's true

———

Until we're unidentified
With any single thing
We'll be locked in fruitless thinking
With an urgency to cling

I'm now open to my magnitude
No limit to this might
Bound to hinder any one or thing
That dims my brilliant light

———

There's no stifling our brilliance
Once we transcend mortal skin
To become one with the universe
And vanquish what has been

———

Once our soul begins advancing
The whole cosmos will be dancing
At a universal ball
Orchestrating one and all

Want and fear live in the mind
But once freed from both we'll find
That pure being is elation
In accord with all creation

———

My blind focus on the future
Clinging fervently to hope
Certain life would grant me riches
Somehow gave me strength to cope
But when wishful dreams proved empty
With illusion laid to rest
I stopped masking pain with promise
And renounced the futile quest

———

Once our fear of death is gone
The sentence ends and we are free
With the universe our channel
To explore exultantly

I've many verses
Left to write
With more despair
Conveyed to light
Forsaken notes
Transposed to songs
And greater good
Derived from wrongs
Much deeper joy
Procured from pain
And empathy
Forged from disdain
True guidance
Granted from above
To light the way
From fear to love

Once I cast off my possessions
The less burdened I became
For acute materiality
And garnering acclaim
Didn't offer what was needed
To obstruct the gaping hole
Just required plunging inward
To restore my ravaged soul

———

Gaining freedom doesn't signify
You've purchased something new
But have made the choice to access
What's already inside you

———

I would rather spend one moment
In the awe of what's unknown
Than waste decades decomposing
In a safe, familiar zone!

When instantly our calendars
Were wiped completely clean
We were thrown into a tailspin
Minus Starbucks and routine
Yet soon came to find this respite
Was a miracle unknown
With the gift of ample time
To spend with family not alone
Ever wiser with the knowledge
Our most treasured wealth indeed
Hails in loving one another
For that's all we truly need

I was taught impassioned praying
Would make all my dreams come true
Disinclined to take a stand
In choosing which path to pursue
Though in living by the precept
To recite my prayers then wait
Watching life unfold by chance
And simply acquiesce to fate
I was powerless to impact
The tomorrows yet to see
And engage in concrete action
To affect my destiny

Once we sever our attachment
To the future and the past
And abandon inclination
Toward delights that never last
We'll soar utterly unfettered
As our souls transcend above
Far beyond all mortal form
Replete with reverence and love

———

I am not afraid of life
And therefore won't belabor death
For the sun will ever shine
Until my last, euphoric breath

———

Do the work you most believe in
And believe in what you do
Then the rest will ring in harmony
At one with all that's true

If only we desired
What we already possessed
Then we wouldn't spend our lifetimes
So materially obsessed

———

It is surely nice to savor
All the riches money buys
Though no value can be placed
On life's most consequential prize

———

We can change the clothes we wear
The place we live and what we do
But our lives will stay the same
Until we change perceptions too

We spend decades masquerading
The facade we wish to be
Shielding every fault and failure
Fear and insecurity
To resemble someone else
Completely free of imperfection
When accepting who we are
Is what enables true connection

———

When we rail against our fate
It doesn't serve the self at all
For we'll never change our plight
And preordained demise forestall
Yet must know that true potential
Lies in hailing what's to be
And transforming sheer despair
Into wholehearted ecstasy

Loss is life's ingenious way
Of making room for what's ahead
Since when grief gives way to trust
We'll access promise there instead

———

No matter how they think
Or what they rashly say and do
They will never take a heart
That proudly beats forever true

———

They may try to take our dignity
In spurning conduct past
But will never touch our souls
Free to transcend aspersions cast

I went searching
For the answers
Blindly racing
Far and wide
When the pathway
To enlightenment
Was waiting
Right inside

———

What you strive to seek then find
Is not invincible or true
For real happiness springs forth
From what was never lost in you

———

If all the wisdom in my head
Could migrate to my heart instead
I'd live each day courageously
With mind absolved and spirit free

I'm the single cloud
That drifts across
A crystal clear blue sky
I'm the tendril
That won't stay
Inside a hair bun piled high
I'm the dandelion
Growing through
The crack in a stone wall
I'm the oak leaf
Vibrant orange
Amidst others green till fall
I'm the black sheep
In the meadow
The pear in the apple bowl
Yet rejoice
In my uniqueness
As a brave, authentic soul

Until we break the pattern
Of behaviors early learned
Through awareness of their ills
And impact on all those concerned
By electing to act differently
Deliberately intent
To ameliorate the past
And further injury prevent
We'll repeat the same mistakes
With no real opportunity
To improve our daily conduct
And set future victims free

———

We possess a superpower
Kept sequestered from plain sight
As most tend to hide their viewpoints
When peer pressure wields its might
Yet must never acquiesce
To disapproval in the fray
When we owe it to ourselves
To let pure instinct guide the way

Once we step outside our prisons
Blazing trails to new frontiers
Throwing caution to the wind
Despite our ever-present fears
Then we'll surely come to see
That we innately had the will
To embark on bold adventures
And our destiny fulfill

———

In adulthood we're quite apt
To leave our inner child behind
When a sense of obligation
Leaves us toiling and confined
And must pledge ourselves to fueling
That which brings us joy each day
Or succumb to deep despair
Since life is bleak when absent play

You needn't stop your thinking
Just attachment to all thought
For the freedom that ensues
Will grant salvation ever sought

———

Once we move beyond our clinging
To the sorrows of the past
We'll create a novel world
Awash in beauty unsurpassed

———

If we focus on the here and now
And disregard the rest
Then each day becomes more wondrous
Than we ever would have guessed

I will not capitulate
To others disinclined to care
Letting scorn destroy my spirit
And submerge me in despair
And must banish recollection
Of betrayals from the past
Now resolved to serve myself
And find tranquility at last

———

Life's objective is to find
Our innate book that writes itself
Or our opus that resounds
From instruments upon a shelf
Or our landscape illustrating
On a canvas from blank space
Or our sculpture emanating
From a mountain's granite face
For that spark inside us yearns
To rise and manifest its light
Though requires sheer intention
To ensure it dazzles bright

Today I saved a life
Although it was my very own
Which won't serve a greater purpose
Till I rescue lives unknown

———

I was solely outcome driven
With results deemed black or white
Some days wallowing in anguish
Others basking in delight
Yet a hostage to perfection
Left me serving time in jail
With no courage to take risks
Or the capacity to fail
Till at last I welcomed grays
To flow amid the other two
For there's nothing more profound
Than living life in every hue

What within us needs attending
So our souls begin ascending?
Just the heart that craves connecting
Or the mind that wants respecting?
Maybe grief that seeks expressing
Or mistakes that take confessing?
Perhaps rage that calls for taming
Or the ego that keeps shaming?
Is it fears that need revealing
Or rejection that seeks healing?
Simple dreams that yearn to fly
Or the conscience asking why?
For wherever we shine light
Terror cannot wield its might
As exposure sets us free
Bound by solidarity

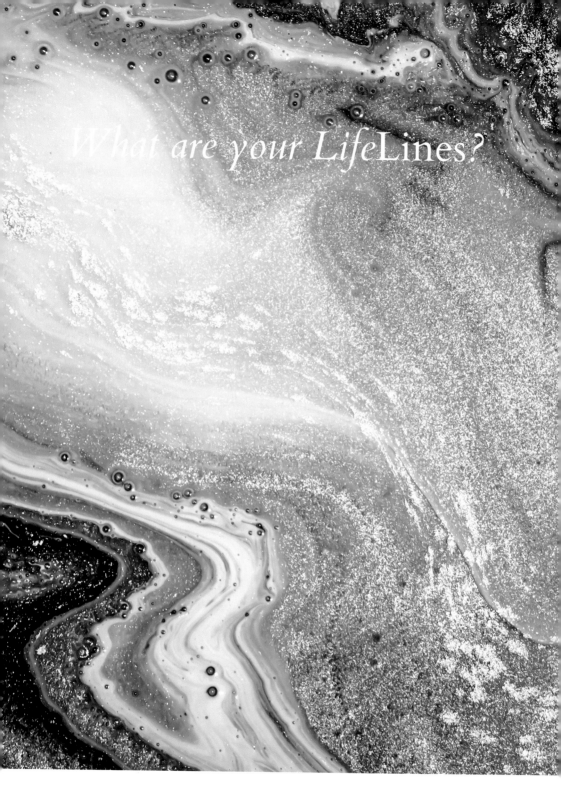

What are your LifeLines?

I would not be here today without my *Life*Lines, as they have granted me the fortitude to survive in a world both beautiful and terrifying, filling me with hope for what lies ahead. In fact, it is with profound awe and gratitude that I can confidently say *"I am thankful to be here and have found innumerable reasons to live."* Although I still vacillate between highs and lows with every day an adventure, I allow, accept and embrace ALL of life as part of the human experience. Today I am intent on making the most of my remaining time and developing deeper bonds with my six uniquely special children, building on my relationship with Doug who has been by my side for 35 years, and forging authentic connections with others embarking on their journeys to self-awareness. I also know it is vital to enlist my *Life*Lines and engage in a daily practice of self-discovery, self-compassion, and self-nurture to live fully and be my best. In fact, our greatest life mission is to journey inward and discover our own essential *Life*Lines. I look forward to sharing with you the candid ups and downs of my ongoing journey, and would be honored to share in yours as well. Please write me your stories, **struggles and** strategies as you seek a pathway to inner peace!

*I truly cannot wait to hear about **your** personal Life**Lines!*

Melissa

EMAIL: MelissaBernstein@*Life*Lines.com
WEBSITE: www.*Life*Lines.com
INSTAGRAM: @seek*Life*Lines

I am thankful Mother Nature
Has become my dearest friend
For it's hidden in her depths
I'm flush with freedom to transcend

Please enjoy these personal photos of my
favorite wonders of nature that astound
and inspire me every day!

Melissa